Ethiopian Discourse

TEODROS KIROS

ETHIOPIAN DISCOURSE

The Red Sea Press, Inc.
Publishers & Distributors of Third World Books

P. O. Box 1892
Trenton, NJ 08607

P. O. Box 48
Asmara, ERITREA

The Red Sea Press, Inc.
Publishers & Distributors of Third World Books

P. O. Box 1892   P. O. Box 48
Trenton, NJ 08607   Asmara, ERITREA

Copyright © 2011 Teodros Kiros
First Printing 2011

Book and cover design: Saverance Publishing Services

Library of Congress Cataloging-in-Publication Data

Kiros, Teodros, 1951-
  Ethiopian discourse / Teodros Kiros.
     p. cm.
   ISBN 1-56902-333-6 (hardcover) -- ISBN 1-56902-334-4 (pbk.) 1. Ethiopia--Politics and government--1991- 2. Democracy--Ethiopia. 3. Political culture--Ethiopia. I. Title.
   DT388.K57 2010
   963.07'2--dc22
                         2010032051

I dedicate this book to my deceased mother Alemsehai, Gebre Mariam my deceased sister, Arsema Mesfin, and my deceased brother, Solomon Kiros whom I loved deeply and who established all my contacts in Ethiopia, during my frequent visits.

CONTENTS

ACKNOWLEDGEMENTS

I must thank my committed publisher Kassahun Checole, who has faith in my work and has to date published all my important philosophical work, and my work as a novelist. I am most grateful to him.

I must also thank Damola Ifaturoti, the senior editor who prevailed over my book on Zara Yacob and this present book with such care and devotion as well as Chris Stites who helped tremendously in the editing and composition, even contributing his own name to the acknowledgments.

I also thank Mary Dooley for her meticulous proofreading. Senait Kassahun helped me in ways which I cannot adequately describe.

I thank Amare Aregawi, the editor of the *Ethiopian Reporter*, who published the essays as weekly columns for five years. I also thank the editor of *Deki Alula*, where I had a weekly column where I developed the ideas on development for five years. Finally I thank Teocla Hagos, editor of *TecolaHagos.com* and Abraha Belay, editor of *Ethiomedia* for publishing the essays on Ethiopian matters.

Irele Abiola, Kwasi Wiredu, Paget Henry and Lewis Gordon's friendships have contributed to my maturity as a scholar and human being; I thank them dearly for attending to all my needs in these long years and lonely years of struggle.

Finally, my years of affiliation with Harvard's African and African American studies and The Du Bois Institute continues to be a source of joy and challenge. I thank Henry Louis Gates, a devoted supporter of my Scholarship.

INTRODUCTION

Ethiopian Discourse is a text which makes heroic efforts to engage the readers with the problems, challenges and traditions of classical and modern Ethiopia.

The book is written for a wide audience. For the past fifteen years, the author takes on Ethiopian topics as they unfolded in and commented on them, challenged the policies of the existing regime. Some of the essays marveled at the idea of revolutionary democracy, when it was freshly introduced to Ethiopian thinking. Like many Ethiopians, the author was at first profoundly impressed by the promises of the regime in power. Hope fueled the writer's imagination, and he wrote about revolutionary democracy admiringly. However, no condition is permanent. When the ruling regime began changing, his writings also change. They become bitter, disappointed and marred by hopelessness. The essays of the new period reflect this mood.

The themes that I take on are both analytic and suggestive. For example the essays on Famine and the developmental state are gratefully informed by the penetrating works of Professor Ghelawdeos Araia who has written enduring essays which will stand the fire of time. In this regard I note that his "Reflections on 'African Development: Dead Ends and New Beginnings' (August 25, 2006) paradigm shift from neo-liberal to a 'democratic developmental state. This work defends government intervention in the economy and the prioritization of rural development, by compellingly arguing that government created rent does not necessarily have to be socially wasteful, except when self-interested maximizing individuals use it to create wealth at the expense of the underprivileged.

His classical analyses of famine in such works such as;

1. *The Politics of Famine and Strategies for Development in Ethiopia*, Doctoral Dissertation, Teachers College, Columbia University, 1990
2. "The paradox of Breadbasket Starving Ethiopia" www.ethiopiafirst.com/news, September 10, 2002
3. "Uprooting the Root Causes of Famine in Ethiopia" www.ethiopiafirst.com/news, November 4, 2002
4. "Famine Could be Defeated Through a Synergy of Development Program," www.dekialula.com, December 4, 2002 are historical masterpieces by a "sagacious thinker".

So are the honest and historically rich writings of Professor Tecola Hagos. With his enviable and courageous writings he continues to leave for us masterful analysis of the Ethiopian condition. I remain grateful to his teachings.

Ethiopian Discourse is really a distillation of what these mighty Ethiopian scholars have taught me. My contribution is simply that of a traveler, a bee, which produces honey by visiting as many flowers as it can, and then extracting the sweetest synthetic whole. Unlike the gifted bee, my contributions are indeed meek, but I think I have made the effort to encourage the introduction of the essay form as the media through which our Ethiopian readers could be informed, enlightened and taught.

If I have achieved anything at all, it is this. The many topics I have written about could be revisited by the growing young generation of writers with fresh insights, and new visions. My dream is to stimulate the Ethiopian imaginary to collect its writings and immortalize them in a book form for the next generation.

1

A Radical Democratic Ethiopian Personality

There is what I call an Ethiopian personality of a classical form. Such Ethiopian personality is wedded to the lineaments of Ethiopian history. This Ethiopian is conscious that her homeland is the birthplace of humankind, that her ancestors built the magnificent civilization at Axum, sculpted gigantic churches out of stone, invented the idea of Christianity, gave the world its first coins, and in the 17th century, witnessed the birth of Zara Yacob (see essay nos. 37 and 40) one of the founders of modern philosophy in the African soil.

The classical Ethiopian personality is a sophisticated historical being. Her moral organization is an outline of historical consciousness and geographical presence of the lush and green of the Ethiopian land. A radical democratic Ethiopian could constructively draw out this classical framework that envelops an Ethiopian personality.

Whereas the brutalities of slavery and the menace of colonialism have inflicted heavy psychological and physical blows to African soil and body, the bravura and will of classical Ethiopians defended Ethiopian sovereignty, with brilliant military prowess at Adwa in 1896. The battle of Adwa is a symbolic source of pride for every Ethiopian and African.

The inferiority complexes forced on Africans everywhere were systematically prevented from insinuating themselves with the Ethiopian personality. This process of invisibility to which black bodies were subjected was countered by the visibility of Ethiopians in world history. This is a great legacy of proud and heroic people. We must draw from this potent historical fountain. We must fertilize our region more attentively. We must replenish it with the best values of modernity, particularly, the modernity of Zara Yacob, our philosophical and spiritual father.

Classical Ethiopian personality was rich in historical awareness and military potency, but was deficient in its respect of the individual as an independent source of knowledge and insight. The modern radical democrat must correct this deficiency. The respect for the dignity and mind of the individual is a distinctly modern idea. The *Hatatas* of Zara Yacob celebrate the individual intelligence and dignity to a degree never heard of in classical Ethiopian history. It is Zara Yacob who introduced this original gene to Ethiopian discourse.

Thinking for oneself, sensitivity to ones' surroundings, questioning the bases of every belief, recognizing the limitations of human thought unsupported by a transcendental power inscribed in the human heart, a prayerful attitude to the wisdom giver inside—all are dimensions of radical modernity, which the classical Ethiopian personality must embrace.

Whereas classical Ethiopian personality specialized in mastering military strategies of defending sovereignty, little attention was paid to enlightening the nation by freeing the individual from tutelage to tradition and high priests. The radical democratic Ethiopian must correct this excess of tradition and hero worship. Tradition has its place in the construction of values that empower the individual. Tradition, however, should not displace the power of reason. Tradition can work in concert with reason. The virtues of the classical Ethiopian personality can work hand in hand with the modern values of a radically democratic Ethiopian.

FROM

The Ethiopian Reporter, March 3, 2002.

2

AFRICA IS NOT HOPELESS; ETHIOPIA IS HOPEFUL

Hopelessness is an existential disposition that poignantly afflicts individuals. An individual suffers from hopelessness in solitude. Hopelessness is accompanied by dread and anxiety. Sometimes individuals commit suicide when they conclude that their situation is hopeless. Sometimes, though one feels hopeless, one is still hopeful. The individual reasons that his plight is temporary, that he need not despair, but strategize patiently.

Groups and continents on the other hand cannot be defined as hopeless in the above existential sense. To be sure, isolated individuals inside them experience their plight existentially. Continents are not hopeless. They can be poor or rich, exploited or exploit others, poorly or richly managed, deprived or blessed with able leaders, lacking in technology or suffused with it. Africa as a continent then is not hopeless, but is gravely mismanaged, in need of scientific and technological facilities. Indeed as *The Economist* pointed out,

> Since January, Mozambique and Madagascar have been deluged by floods, famine has started to reappear in Ethiopia, Zimbabwe has succumbed to government-sponsored thuggery, and poverty and pestilence continue unabated. Most seriously, wars still rage from north to south and east to west. No one can blame Africans for the weather, but most of the continent's shortcomings owe less to acts of God than to acts of man. These are not exclusively African—brutality, despotism and corruption exist everywhere—but African societies, for reasons buried in their cultures, seem especially susceptible to them. (The Economist, p.17)

The last lines are shockingly provincial and shortsighted, deliberately ignorant of African history. To be sure, there are African leaders who fit the profile. Indeed, they are brutal, despotic, corrupt and much else. However, these are individual attributes provoked and nurtured by the relentless quest for wealth and power. Brutality, despotism and corruption inevitably follow. Despotic leaders are perfectly profiled by Plato in book nine of his *Republic*. Plato immortalized this leader type without data from Africa. For him, these types of leaders are inevitable possibilities of a regime unregulated by reason.

Capital feeds on these attributes, and it is money not culture, that is luring certain African leaders to imbibe these vices of capital. There are many African cultures and practices that have no place for brutality, despotism and corruption. I have described them separately in two different books, *Explorations in African Political Thought* and *Moral Philosophy and Development*. In fact, all too often, these are practices that historically originated in the West, and that certain African leaders consecrate and indigenize as the ethics of success. Are slavery and colonialism less brutal than rape, cannibalism and amputation as *The Economist* seems to imply. Again, was it not certain individuals who were slaveholders and colonialists, or is it the case that the defining essence of the West is slavery and colonialism, and likewise, the defining essence of Africa is brutality, despotism and corruption? Should we not replace essentialism with contingency and irony, since the latter are better tools of understanding human behavior?

Africa is not hopeless. It is mismanaged. Its vast land and huge resources are underutilized partly because its bureaucrats, as their counterparts all over the world, are inept, corrupt, greedy and short-sighted. Killer diseases for millennia have afflicted the continent. The recent discovery of AIDS is memorable only because of its contemporaneity coupled with the fact that it has now become a Western disease.

Otherwise, this so-called dark continent has been dark in the minds of the West for centuries. AIDS, however, is not a manifestation of hopelessness. It is a sign of underdevelopment. It is Africa's agony and anguish. However, the prevalence of AIDS speaks less to hopelessness and more directly to the fact of human indifference, within and outside of Africa. The permanently rich, particularly outside of Africa and inside the United States, continue to command billions of dollars of assets buttressed by huge salaries, and yet they pay blind eyes to the plight of 23 million Africans who are fated to die from AIDS. Medical experts estimate that it would cost the modest amount of $600 a month to attend to the needs of an AIDS patient, and that all that we would need to save some lives of dying children is to raise about $23 billion.

Imagine that we organize an AIDS funding project and that we asked a contribution of $10.00 a month from every willing individual, in no time we would be able to procure the desperately needed money to save lives. The point is simply that Africa's agony and anguish can be solved by money. Its entrenched behavioral practices can then be addressed systematically through protracted educational programs. Even those programs presuppose the existence of funds. African children and their educable parents could then be taught the virtues of self-control, moderation and responsibility by educators—virtues Africans need to insinuate into their everyday lives.

It is shocking that 23 million lives will be wasted like flies, when the rich and comfortable are living the good life, buying and selling expensive homes, buying human organs, having face lifts, drinking $500 bottles of wine, dining at the most expensive restaurants, where they order food they barely touch. These are acts of moral shame. The discrepancy between the lives of the powerful and rich, and the lives of the poor and ill, where 52 percent of African children are fated to die from AIDS, does not manifest hopelessness, but rather reveals the brutal fact that humanity is living in denial, the denial of moral responsibility to help the needy and the unfortunate victims of life. These cruel facts speak to the indifference of the rich and fortunate, to all those sleepwalkers of modernity. Africa's apparent hopelessness is a crisis of moral intelligence.

Of course not all is grave. There are signs of hope everywhere. Africa is hopeful. Uganda has successfully blended toughness with compassionate education and continues to reduce the AIDS epidemic very impressively. Ethiopia and Eritrea have now embraced peace, and at least Ethiopia has avowed to fight its perennial enemy: poverty; South Africa and Zimbabwe have been warned not to live in denial, and to battle AIDS. They owe it to their children, whose parents fought against apartheid to pave a beautiful path for them.

There is even more spectacular news for Ethiopia. The *Financial Times* in its June 22, 2000, edition has reported the heartwarming news. It is one more example that, if Ethiopia and Eritrea embrace a definitive peace, one of the conditions of development will have been satisfied. Peace is a necessary condition for development. Industriousness and spine are juices of development. Peace, industriousness and will are the necessary and sufficient conditions for defeating the war against poverty in Africa. Equipped with the above necessary and sufficient conditions, Ethiopia, at the present, is suitably and energetically situated to be a hope for Africa.

FROM

Africana.com, July 20, 2001.

SOURCES

Teodros Kiros, Ed, *Explorations in African Political Thought* (New York: Routledge, 2000).

Teodros Kiros, *Moral Philosophy and Development: The Human Condition in Africa* (Athens: Ohio University Press, 1992).

Teodros Kiros, *Self-Construction and the Formation of Human Values: Language, Truth and Desire* (Connecticut: Praeger, 1999).

3

TRAGEDY IN OUR MIDST: REMEMBERING THE DEAD ON SEPTEMBER 11ᵀᴴ

I was home on September 11, 2001, writing away, struggling with words, and they were not coming. A shiny and bright day it was. I kept looking outside admiring the scene, grateful to the weather. I kept looking outside in search of ideas to put on paper. Again, nothing was coming. This restlessness continued for two hours. I remember not feeling well when I woke up. I was haunted by a bad dream, in which I was chased the whole night by something. I woke up with that dream. I always begin my day by reading my email, as I did that day. I read a mysterious letter from Harvard University's president that expressed condolences to families, and comforted students about the horrible deaths of innocent lives. I must have been dreaming, for I could not fathom the meaning of the letter. So I casually moved on to read other messages. Business as usual. The telephone rang and it was the voice of my distressed wife, who impatiently asked me if I have heard the news. I said no. She then informed me about the deaths in New York City. I rushed to the TV. There it was. I remained glued to it from September 11th to September 17th. Horror on the screen. A replay of jets that had just monstrously pierced the interiors of the towering buildings which housed the World Trade Center, the landmarks of high modernity, the apogee of technological prowess.

The massive explosion inside had just swallowed human bodies, with the wobbly steel bending and melting away, and the towers collapsing into rubble. Bodies falling away in forms barely distinguishable from shattered concrete and broken steel.

In a faraway corner, a lone photographer's body appears and disappears, struggling to immortalize a historical moment, before it is extinguished in oblivion. I can see his face, sometimes looking at me, the viewer in shock, and then I face his back, as he continues to witness the making of human history, another episode of shameful human action, another production of hate and grief. How ashamed I felt to be human. I wished I wasn't.

Firemen rushing to the scene in record numbers soon became consumed by the inferno. Police rescuing trapped bodies, by forcefully disengaging them from steel and concrete. All of a sudden I am witnessing a war zone, without combatants. The enemies and their victims were consumed by fire and abused by steel.

Pilots, janitors, firefighters, cleaners and many others exploded inside the buildings. I imagined the horrors of their deaths, their last seconds on this cursed planet, their frightened faces looking at the face of God. My ears were deafened by their screams pleading with their killers. I asked myself why, why did this happen? Why do human beings have to die this way? Is it not enough that some of those who died have already been burdened by the weight of existence, by responsibility, duty, bills and unconsummated dreams and diseases?

Some of them woke up at an early hour that day to make beds, to clean offices, to make money that day, like all other days. I felt like saying "Speak God, speak to me!" The bills that they have to pay, the long hours they have to put in to take care of their loved ones, the money that they have sent to their relatives drenched in poverty in faraway places, the future that they had to secure for themselves and their children were not enough burden. They had to be punished with horrible ways of dying.

This should not have been, should not have been. Look how it ended. Now that they are dead, how should we the living remember them? Our immediate reaction is anger, the desire to revenge, if necessary, in a disproportionate way. This is understandable. Indeed, it is the immediate language of anger, of grief. How could it be otherwise? An eye for an eye is the immediate feeling. Anger is indeed a rational reaction to injustice. In this sense, it is just to be angry. After the dust is settled, and this is bound to take the nation a long time, we have to begin reflecting on why this happened. Most specifically, we must address the question of not only what did the "terrorists" want but also what do those whom the terrorists represent want?

FROM

The Ethiopian Reporter, September 26, 2001.

4

RADICAL
DEMOCRATIC VALUES

Equality and freedom are cardinal values. No society in the past, and perhaps not one in the future, could ever be appealing or attractive as a social form to humans if it does not provide freedom and equality.

No matter where, humans will remain interested and will continue to fight for freedom and create and preserve equality for themselves. Any ruler, no matter what his justifications may be, who dares to deny freedom to some and grant it to others, or would treat some as equals and as others as subordinates, may stay in power through intimidation, and sometimes because the time is not right for spontaneous revolt or organized revolution, but not for very long. Most revolutions, beginning with the French revolution, through the Russian and Chinese revolutions, and ending with wars of liberation in the colonies, were fought because the subjects were both unfree and unequal. It is these ideals that started the fire of revolution and revolt.

Freedom and equality are therefore precious democratic values that Ethiopians, like other human beings value enormously. It so happens that modern Ethiopian citizens, in spite of the constitution that abstractly idealizes these values, are treated neither as free nor equal. The constitution has promised them the delivery of freedom and equality. Everyday life in Ethiopia does not reflect the tranquility of freedom and the right of equality. This dangerous situation endangers the bloated Ethiopian state.

The so called hooligans who roam the streets of Addis and the lonely corners of the countryside; the beggars who are rudely whisked away from the crowded streets of the city by well-clad and well-fed men inside shiny European cars; the homeless elders who take shelter in famished churchyards; the overstarved peasants in the countryside who die there from unknown causes; the eleven-year-old AIDS infested prostitutes ready to do anything to merely exist, without hope and purpose; the unemployed idlers of the downtrodden tea houses and their hashish; the proud mothers and fathers who visit one house after the other in search of one meal a day from those who have the heart to give; the shoeshine boys who linger in the sun, all day long fighting angry mosquitoes— all are all human beings waiting for rights, yearning for freedom with dignity. They have heard about these ideals. The newspapers habitually mention them. They have never lived these ideals. They too are human beings. They too are souls with dignity. They too are sources of insight, as philosophy has sung to them. They have been charmed by these intoxicating ideals. But they never lived them as legitimate beings. This miserable reality is marked for explosion one day, unless the sleepy Ethiopian state attends to it immediately and efficiently.

It is normal to hear in Ethiopia that the poor like to beg and steal. This is wrong. Stealing and begging are weapons of the poor. They resort to them after everything else fails. Soon, very soon, Ethiopian legislators must develop concrete principle of justice. I suggest two of them. The current constitution must be amended to add the following:

- All Ethiopians are entitled to basic freedoms—freedom of thought, freedom of movement, freedom of assembly to change things—that must be changed.
- All Ethiopians are entitled to food, shelter, health and clothing; and the appetites of the rich and powerful are not as fundamental as the necessary needs of ordinary Ethiopians.

I have elaborated on these principles of justice in *Moral Philosophy and Development: The Human Conditon in Africa* (Ohio University Press, Athens, Ohio, 1992.)

FROM
The Ethiopian Reporter, March 3, 2002.

5

PORTRAITS OF CHARACTERS WITH INTEGRITY IN AFRICAN NOVELS: A PHILOSOPHICAL REFLECTION

Frantz Fanon, the medical doctor and revolutionary thinker from Martinique wrote, in his *The Wretched of the Earth*:

> The town belonging to the colonized people, or at least the native town, the Negro village, the medina, the reservation, is a place of ill fame, peopled by men of evil repute. They are born there, it matters little where or how; they die there, it matters not where, nor how. It is a world without spaciousness; men live there on top of each other, and their huts are built on top of the other. The native town is a hungry town, starved of bread, of meat, of shoes, of coal, of light. The native town is a crouching village, a town on its knees, a town wallowing in the mire. It is a town of niggers and dirty Arabs. The look that the native turns on the settler's town is a look of lust, a look of envy. (p. 39)

The six novelists I will be discussing—Ayi Kwei Armah, Sembène Ousmane, Buchi Emechta, Nega Mezlekia, Tayeb Salih and Ngugi Wa Thiong'o—respond to this haunting passage, each in his or her own way.

Novels since their very inception have always struggled with issues of moral character. Character has stimulated the philosophical novelist's imaginative moral fiber. Indeed, it is the preoccupation of the novelist with the question of character that brought about the birth of the philosophical novel.

A string of powerful European novels like Albert Camus' *The Stranger* and *The Fall*, Thomas Mann's *Magic Mountain*, Fyodor Dostoyevsky's *The Idiot*, and Jean Paul Sartre's *La Nausee* engaged the theme of integrity. Continuing this well-established tradition, and sometimes influenced by it, African novelists Armah's *The Beautyful Ones Are Not Yet Born*; Sembène's *God's Bits of Wood*; Emecheta's *The Joys of Motherhood*; Mezlekia's *Notes from the Hyena's Belly*; Salih's *Season Of Migration to the North*; and Ngugi's *Matigari* variously and richly address issues of integrity, and passions for truth and justice.

All these novelists are powerful advocates of truth and justice. In their novels they address corruption, justice, truth, war and peace. In *The Beautyful Ones Are Not Yet Born*, Armah's nameless central character referred to as "the man" battles heroically the tempting intrusion of Ghanaian-African corruption into his soul. Corruption follows him everywhere, and the character fights it heroically. His wife and other family members think that he is a fool, a loser to say no to the fortunes of corruption. He shuns them all, by holding fast to his moral ground. Of course, he has doubts, as this passage suggests, but ultimately he holds his ground:

> Visibly, the song deepened the silence of the man on the bed. For the man sitting on the desk opposite, all the cool sadness seemed able to do was to raise thoughts of the lonely figure finding it more and more difficult to justify his own honesty. How could he, when all around him the whole world never tired of saying there were only two types of men who took refuge in honesty—the cowards and the fools? Very often these days he was burdened with the hopeless, impotent feeling that he was not just one of these, but a hopeless combination of the two. (p. 51)

The African world around him is teeming with corruption, sprawling with shameless men corrupting their souls. The man's children thought that their father was a fool to spurn wealth and power. The man's ideal of the moral firmament above him in the sky was his lodestar. The Ghanaian world outside worshipped the gods of wealth, lies and power. Those were the toxins that the man's upright character jettisoned to his family's scolding response. The man felt like a failed poet. His eternal curse was that he had no followers, no admirers, not even among the youngest. They had all gone crazy with money and power. He and his hopeless ideals shone like a flickering candle in the middle of the night: alone, forgotten, lighting itself to death.

In a dark political atmosphere of 1947-48 West Africa's Dakar, Sembène, Armah's traveling companion, encountered workers staging a momentous strike on the Dakar-Niger railway that shook Senegal's weak and sickly state, a state long founded on the colonial pillars of relentless oppression of working people. *In God's Bits of Wood*, Sembene Ousmane, Senegal's leading novelist, tells us a moving story of passion for justice through the character of Penda, a heroine, who took up the prohibiting task of demanding justice for Senegalese workers:

> The women of Dakar, those tireless vendors in the shantytowns of Dakar, in the "natives quarters" had been forced to sell everything they owned of any value and they were beginning to be disturbed by the lack of buyers. It was impossible now to find a market for their best head cloths or for the waistcloths or fine cotton from the most highly skilled weavers of the city, which had been the symbol of their virginity and were the pride of the entire family. The merchants were turning down even the rarest fetishes—those which protected their owner from the evil eye and turned away the Jinn and any other form of misfortune. (p. 86)

In direct contrast to the abysmal reality, like Fanon before him, Sembene gives us a portrait of the "settler's town." The European settlers had it easy. They lived luxuriously:

> The villas of the European employees of the company stood in a district, well outside the city proper, which Lahib—without knowing quite why—had once christened "the Vatican." The houses themselves were all alike, with prefabricated roofs, well-kept lawns, graveled walks, and porches surrounded by a low cement railing....Life was easy in the "Vatican"—so easy that it became extremely monotonous, and the adults all seemed to have taken on that scrawling, sullen appearance which is the hallmark of boredom. The strike,

however, had changed the atmosphere considerably; a constant nervous tension hung in the air, and fear was mingled with normal irritability. (p. 162)

Similarly, Buchi Emecheta in the *Joys of Motherhood* addresses the myriad concerns of Nigerian women. The novel is a celebration of the joys of motherhood, in spite of the hardships of the duty of mothering, in the Nigerian context that sets men free in the name of tradition. Emecheta's women are invariably proud, unfailingly sacrificing and specifically selfless. They live and work for their children. It is that burning desire to raise successful children that anchors these women's existence. The Nigerian women in the novel have become strong, proud and stubbornly arrogant. These are traits of survival that they have developed to deal with their self-loving men. For Emecheta, modernity has produced particular kinds of Nigerian men whom she describes accurately. Modernity, she argues, has trampled upon the traditional beauty of village life, most particularly love relations. In one poignant moment, she writes:

> Like other husbands and wives in Lagos, Nnu Ego and Nuaife started growing slightly apart, not that they were that close at the start. Now each was in a different world. There was no time for petting or talking to each other about love. That type of family awareness which the illiterate farmer was able to show his wives, his household, his compound, had been lost in Lagos, for the job of shiny trinkets. Few men in Lagos would have time to sit and admire their wives' tattoos, let alone tell them tales of animals nestling in the forests, like the village husband who might lure a favorite wife into the farm to make love to her with only the sky as their shelter, or bathe in the same stream with her, scrubbing one another's backs. (p. 52)

In this passage, the sad novelist announces the end of love, the death of passion. The modern city has become the site of emptiness, calculation and business. There love has no place. The city is intoxicated with money and all its trappings. Corruption, prostitution, lies, murder and rape are the ways of enriching oneself. That is how difference and distinctions are produced by desire without passion. The actors are corrupt politicians and the greedy businessmen. Surely, they have lots of time for quick sex to contain their anxiety, but have no time for love. They would tell you there is no love. Everything is sex.

"The new men are machines," argues Emecheta. "Loving and caring is difficult for them." In contrast to these men, her women are passionate, caring, engaged and deep. They invest in mother-hood, and make themselves like it. Women like Nnu Ego are born to serve their children. They work until the bitter end of time. Even in death, they find no rest, laments Emecheta.

Nega Mezlekia's contribution to the philosophical novel is his near perfect anatomy of war and death, through an autobio-graphical description of his coming of age in modern Ethiopia. *Notes from the Hyena's Belly*, documents the horrors of war and the ravages of starvation and famine. The reader is told, "We children lived like the donkey, careful not to wonder off the beaten trail and end up in the Hyena's belly." Everyday life was uncertain in this world. No one knew that he or she could stay alive at the end of the day. The communist liberators who took over Ethiopia were everything but decent men of integrity. They were obsessed with war and death. They killed for no reason, but simply because others had a different vision.

All these novelists are responding directly to the colonial experience. Bitter as the African social reality is and however deeply scarred its victims, none of these novelists captures the hopelessness of colonial reality. They all sought to transcend it novelistically, by creating hopeful characters.

Tayeb Salih goes in the opposite direction. First, however, he too idealizes the precolonial past as idyllic and positive and he paints with the brushes of transcendence. In the world-famous *Season of Migration to the North*, Salih captures North African reality with remarkable perfection—perfection of an evil charac-ter, sculpted in colonial waters.

On the one hand, his characters are rooted in Africa's humane precolonial past. The narrator writes, "I felt not like a storm-swept feather but like that palm tree, a being with a background with roots, with a purpose" (p. 2). Salih strives to establish a common root for all human beings. He creates a universal context for us all. After all, we are told we are all the same, the children of common geography and common ancestry. We all dream, grow and die. No human being is spared of this reality. The only difference is that we die at different times. Time marks our disappearance from this space. That is all. Otherwise,

> From the cradle, to the grave, they dream dreams, some of which come true and some of which are frustrated; that they fear the unknown, search for love and seek contentment in wife and child; that some are strong and some are weak; that some have been given more than they deserve by life, while others have been deprived by it, but the differences are narrowing and most of the weak are no longer weak. (p. 3)

That is human reality, in which all of us are potentially ground.

Remembering the precolonial past, Salih imagines life around the banks of the Nile as teeming with the movement of time and the change of space. He remembers the paths of time on our memory, marking the past, the present and the future. He imagines the tree he saw in the village changing, the bank of the Nile retreating. He sees the city of Cairo rife with crowds. He sees life giving and taking. He hears a bird singing, a dog barking, wood and axe making sound. Life is sometimes stable. He remembers his grandfather telling him stories about heroes of the distant past. All these things make him whole, complete, stable like the root of a sturdy tree.

The stability however does not last long. He is violated by colonial reality. His tradition is subjugated. He is made invisible. His past is erased. All of a sudden he feels unstable. His roots are shaken. Everything changes. He above all changes.

His central character, Mustafa, is a product of the violent change. His integrity is shattered. He grows into a monster. Resentful and violent, he goes after white women. He does not love. He makes them fall in love. Then at the heat of ecstasy they are killed, erased from time and space.

Mustafa Saed declares Salih, "was the most brilliant student of our day." He was the first to marry an Englishwoman, a European. Soon, he turns into a savage killer. With a razor-sharp mind, he seduces woman after woman. Then he kills them. This is his revenge against the queens of the west.

The novels of Ngugi wa Thiong'o interrogate the nature of truth. All his characters take on unjust institutions. As Ngugi put it, "The true seeker of justice never loses hope. The true seeker of justice never tires...Truth must seek justice" (*Matigari*, p. 84).

It is precisely the decadent colonial institutions that cultivated the absolutely resentful Mustafa in the haunting pages of *Season of Migration to the North*. It is the death of those institutions that Ngugi calls for through his justly powerful character Matigari.

All his writings—beginning with the youthful short stories in *Secret Lives*, through his masterpiece, *Weep Not Child*, to his very well seasoned *Matigari*—are passionate cries for justice and speaking truth to power. His characters are piercing, fearless and intelligent visionaries.

For Ngugi, only a being with superhuman qualities can save the corrupt African world. That person is Matigari. His readers do not know his sex, gender, age or life history. All that we know is that he has drunk from the vessel of justice and is burning with it. Like Plato's philosopher-king, this "superbeing" wants to change the world, through the power of words. Soon, however, he discovers that words are not enough. He needs agency.

Matigari fervently believed in values such as that the products of labor must be owned by the laborers, that renters should own the houses they live in (p.74). Throughout his travels and the people he met, he did not find a single just person. Matigari

> was saddened because he bore a burden of many unanswered questions, which he turned in his mind alone. What frightened him was the feeling that he was perhaps the only one preoccupied with what was happening in the country, indeed, as if he was alone in the entire country...he looked for truth and justice in the grass and in the bushes. He searched among the thorns, in the shrubs, the ditches and the molehills, and in birds' nests. He searched for them in the whole of nature. (p. 86)

He found justice nowhere, neither in nature nor in human deeds. He was hurt by the discovery of this fact of our existence. He looked everywhere, spoke to power holders, to the poor, to the marginalized. The powerful held him in contempt for harassing them in questions. They indicted him for madness. His madness, they argued, is manifest in the values that he is imposing on society. Only the mad think that the laborer should own his products, and that renters should not pay rent but own only the places they live in.

He was arrested and imprisoned. Matigari, however escapes prison, and becomes a revolutionary. Matigari argues that the world cannot be changed by words only. Words are indispensable as vehicles of critical thought to speak to the world, to write for the world, when one can. Justice and truth, however, must be imposed on the world through words strengthened by arms. As Matigari put it, "Justice for the oppressed springs from the organized armed power of the people" (p. 8).

The African novel is born out of struggle. Anguish, pain, the abuse of the soul and the body, partly ground in colonial history, and partly ground in human weakness, infuse the novelists' imagination. Few novelists can free themselves from history's barbaric intrusion.

The novelists I discuss here are all marred by this history. They wrote their novels both as a document and an exercise in imaginative freedom. The contours of the African world, expansive and huge as they may be, are forced by history to politicize the novel. Hence, the rise of the political novel from the African soil.

Justifying his trade, Ngugi writes, "As I write I remember the nights of fighting in my father's house; my mother's struggle with the soil so that we might eat, have decent clothes and get some schooling....I remember the fears, the betrayals, the moments of despair and love and kinship in struggle and I try to find the meaning of it all through my pen" (*Secret Lives*, Introduction).

Ngugi speaks for all the major African novelists. For the novelists I chose to study here, the novel is a vehicle of self-exploration, a disclosure of the particular, through which the universal drama of the human condition in Africa is exposed. In this way, the African novelist is a secret agent.

Of course the experiences vary. Kenya, Ghana, Nigeria, the Sudan are separate nations, with unique experiences. But all of them have been essentialized by the badge of slavery and the barbarism of colonialism. The African novel documents that experience, and seeks to change it through ideal characters that seek to change that world by creating upright and decent beings.

FROM

The Ethiopian Reporter, April 4, 2002.

SOURCES

Frantz Fanon, *The Wretched of the Earth* (New York: Grove Press, 1965).

Ayi Kwei Armah, *The Beautyful Ones Are Not Yet Born* (London: Heinemann) 1968.

Sembène Ousmane, *God's Bits of Wood* (London: Heinemann, 1962).

Buchi Emecheta, *Joys of Motherhood* (New York: Braziller, 1979).

Nega Mezlekia, *Notes from the Hyena's Belly* (New York: Picador, 2000).

Tayeb Salih, *Season of Migration to the North* (London: Heinemann, 1969).

Ngugi Wa Thiong'o, *Matigari* (London: Heinemann, 1987).

Ngugi Wa Thiong'o, *Secret Lives* (London: Heinemann, 1964).

Ngugi Wa Thiong'o, *Weep Not Child* (London: Heinemann, 1964).

6

DEMOCRACY AND TOLERANCE

Tolerance is to democracy as passion is to love. Surely, we can pretend that we are in love without passion. Indeed, as is most often the case, we feign passion, so as to appear to be in love; similarly, we equally and shamelessly invoke democracy without the disposition of tolerance, so as to appear seamlessly democratic.

These pretensions, however, are dangerous. Too many dreams have been shattered; too many values crushed before they developed roots; too many unnecessary wars have been fought in Ethiopian history—only because we feign tolerance without believing in it, or worse still, we simply do not tolerate that which we do not like, so long as we can obliterate it from the face of the earth.

Intolerance is one of the pitfalls of Ethiopian culture. It always has been. Sadly, the culture has progressively worsened with democratic socialism, a blend of traditional Ethiopian authoritarianism and vulgar Marxist totalitarianism. Authoritarianism and totalitarianism are the archenemies of radical democracy, and through them, tends the idea of tolerance.

Intolerance is the highest form of arrogance. Arrogance is the most pernicious way of belittling individual intelligence, precisely because the arrogant person does not think anything that is worth her time exists outside of her self-enclosing self. To assume that nothing exists outside oneself is to decide that one does not have to take the other person who is speaking, feeling and attempting to say something as worth the arrogant person's time. This assumption results in both insulating the arrogant person from learning something different from another person, and vitiating the ignored person from flourishing as an individual by confidently practicing the values she so intimately knows. She is not even asked what she thinks. She is simply dismissed as a self without source, a self without being.

Through these techniques of exclusion of values, voices and hearts of real individuals the world is denied access to the plenitude of the vast world of diverse values and the individuals who bear them. Intolerance then takes the subtle and not so subtle form of selective listening and selective appreciation of human values. We tolerate only that which is closest to us, or that which resembles our own values and customs.

Our leaders in particular have perfected intolerance as a way of life. In fact, their brand of democracy, which they call democratic centralism, has elevated intolerance as a necessary moment cratic ocracy. This view is wrong. If democracy means anything er mean tolerating ways of doing things, ways of speaking. There are so many ways of crossing a arriving at a decision.

ved at many meet- to qualify to par- as to always agree ne such dogmatic rcle who secretly sion down the throats of the member dares to question this premise, his days are numbered. First, he is isolated; second, he is ridiculed; third he is given warnings; fourth, he is dismissed; fifth, if he persists to criticize, from the outside, he will be obliterated.

FROM

The Ethiopian Reporter, April 4, 2002.

7

REASON AND DEMOCRACY

The inner voice directs secretly. The heart is the home of that voice. It discloses itself only to the most deserving, and that takes place when the self is free to focus, and is willing to be guided. The encounter between reason and the anxious self—because it is confused, but willing to be instructed—takes place at special moments.

In normal time, and within the institutions of ordinary democracy, reason takes a back seat. It is engaged in self-centered bargaining, calculations and life plans. Humans in such times, as we learned from Plato, become busybodies. Desire runs amok. Restless search for commodities becomes a way of life.

Restlessness is hostile to the environment that the summoning of inner reason demands from us. Inner peace, the willingness to receive, the readiness for self-searching, requires absolute quiet. Stillness and disengagement from the everyday world are absolute prerequisites for the revelation of insights from our inner power, our reasoning power, hidden inside the human heart.

Of course we all have to make a living in one way or another. That is an obvious necessity. We Ethiopians as well, probably more than others, because of the economic situation in our country, are harassed by the contingencies of life. Our obligations outweigh our means. I have witnessed the weight of responsibility when I go to my homeland, and stay at my parents' home, those poor people's eyes that meet me in the compound. Malnourished toddlers on their mother's backs struggling to smile at me, lifeless eyes, emaciated bodies of mothers and fathers, deciding between feeding themselves and their children, the proud elders coming with gifts to home, hoping to be paid for them. These daily realities of Ethiopian life for the poor shrink and depress my heart with the weight of responsibility.

My homeland is burning with poverty and disease. Yet, I the radical democrat do not know what to do. Of course, I should know what to do. I must consult my heart. Ordinary democracy does not challenge me enough. Surely, it has successfully trained me to make money, to take care of myself and perhaps my family. I now know that I can make billions of dollars. Our Ethiopian millionaires are well schooled at that.

Ordinary democracy justifies my greed, my selfishness. It tells me that life is short, nasty and brutish. All my vices are justified as natural. Radical democracy challenges ordinary liberal democracy, by arguing that we can remake man, redesign him up to a point. Years of uncritical socialization to the ideas of ordinary liberal democracy have to be rethought.

An intelligent Ethiopian cannot afford to cushion himself on the pillows of liberal democracy. We Ethiopians cannot ignore the weight of responsibility and the demands of moral obligation. The radical Ethiopian democrat must return to the roots of democracy. She has to refashion herself, redesign dead institutions anchored on the vulgarity of totalitarian socialism and callous liberal capitalism. We must find another way. We must construct a third way, relevant to the Ethiopian condition. A new Ethiopian personality has to be reconstructed.

FROM

The Ethiopian Reporter, March 3, 2002

8

BEYOND ETHNICITY AND NATIONALISM: NATIONAL CONSCIOUSNESS

All Ethiopians can be taught to admire our differences as members of historically generated ethnic groups and as thinking beings, as beings born with the "capacity to think." We can be re-taught to trust more and not less, to expunge from the fibers of our being the poison of suspicion and forced unanimity. We Ethiopians should learn how not to hide behind artificial nationalism, a nationalism that does not allow us to freely and courageously criticize our leaders when they make shameful mistakes in our name. As beings with the capacity to think, we must use this power to peacefully challenge our leaders when they fail to carry out the tasks that we mandated them to perform.

The Ethiopian people should not be used as pawns the government consults only when they are in trouble. That is treason. It is immoral and politically suicidal. Ethiopians should be permitted to participate in the construction of their nation. Instead, the nationalism and internationalism of Meles Zenawi is used destructively, to maintain the position of those in power. Power need not be used as Bonapartism, as Meles shrewdly alleges is the way that the dissidents are using it. One could convincingly argue that Bonapartism is double-pronged, that he himself is as guilty of it as any of his critics.

But these attacks and counterattacks are useless in the end as I argue in "When Two Elephants Fight It Is the Grass That Suffers" (see next essay). Meles should forge a new Ethiopia blessed by the beauty and diversity of a multi-ethnic state. A multiethnic state, however, must be delinked from negative ethnicity, as I argue in "Two Concepts of Ethnicity" (essay no. 39).

An authentic multiethnic state is not nationalistic. Its base ought to be morally educated citizens. Political consciousness is not enough. Political consciousness must wrap itself with moral consciousness. For years, all over the world, particularly in the homelands of vulgar Marxism, citizens have been falsely told that political parties could politically educate them. That is a lie; a shameless lie at that. Nobody can educate another easily. Citizens can educate themselves as moral subjects if they are given the appropriate public sphere, so that they can boldly use their own "public reason." The idea of belonging or not belonging to a nation cannot be taught from the outside. One cannot be told to love one's nation because one is born to it or, more mendaciously, because one's kin and blood relations or its race constructed it.

We know too well that this is what gullible citizens are told all over the world, to their detriment. Indeed, that is how individuals all over the world are politically miseducated. But it need not be that way, not inexorably. Nothing is permanent. This false sense of belonging, which is what nationalism feeds on, contrary to what some political scientists teach at universities, and which some media writers dignify in their nicely written columns, is neither the complete picture nor carefully thought out. Or, when it is ostensibly worked out, it is done with the end purpose of disenabling the potentially conscious citizen to think for himself or herself.

The leader worthy of that name, takes it upon himself or herself, to demask this process of moral and political miseducation. The leader as a teacher gently not manipulatively heightens the awareness of the citizens through a subtle transformation from nationalism, as an irrational love of the idea of the nation, to national consciousness, as a morally acute sense of the nation. It is the duty of the leader, when called upon, to introduce citizens to the differences between nationalism and consciousness about belonging to a nation.

Rarely, however, are these feelings distinguished for the dizzy citizens smearing the dirt of negative ethnicities, the cousins of narrow nationalism. Where there is no functional government guided by the idea of national consciousness, the true leader provides one. If the existing nation is marred by nationalism and negative ethnicity, the leader replaces that false sense of belonging with a truer one. As Fanon put the matter in *The Wretched of the Earth*, the duty of those at the head of the movement is to have the masses behind them. Allegiance presupposes awareness and understanding of the mission that has to be fulfilled; in short, an intellectual position, however embryonic. We must not voodoo the people, nor dissolve them in emotion and confusion (pp. 199-200). Furthermore, Fanon stresses, "A government which calls itself a national government ought to take responsibility for the totality of the nation" (p. 201).

The present situation in Ethiopia requires the services of a leader who must educate the party he leads and the people who follow him. He must teach again and again. He must not resort to butchery and manipulation when he cannot exact consent and consensus through the art of persuasion. He must free the people from the voodoo of negative ethnicity, intoxication with nationalism, hate and confusion over the direction that the nation should follow. At issue is the perennial question of what a nation is. A nation is composed of individuals with diverse desires and aspirations.

Some of these desires and aspirations are so distinct that they resist the idea of forging a common good to which, when necessary, they have to be sacrificed. Living within a nation of morally and politically conscious individuals requires the creation of a common good. A good is common when it has something that all the citizens should have, before they can be left free to realize their distinct desires and aspirations. Food, health, shelter and clothing are fundamental goods that all Ethiopian citizens should have, before others who can and should have more are encouraged to do so.

The common good as the good consisting of health, food, shelter and clothing should not be perceived as coercive, however. The idea of national consciousness should insinuate itself into the moral fibers of individual Ethiopian citizens as a duty. The morally and politically conscious Ethiopians ought not to feel constrained when their government gently guides them to think for others, to embrace the needs of those who live in tin shacks as their very own responsibility to ameliorate. This sense of responsibility has to be created by any means necessary.

In modern Ethiopia this good must be distributed by a responsible state to all Ethiopians, and not to particular ethnic groups. National consciousness is embodied in the imperative that the dignity of all Ethiopians should not be the plaything of manipulative politicians who exploit the politics of blood relations and kin.

Nationhood is too precious to simply and plainly be an attribute of nationalism. The future Ethiopian state can come into being only as an activity of national consciousness propelled by an impartial wisdom of a leader mobilizing the resources of a functional state. Ethiopia at the moment is yearning for both.

FROM

The Ethiopian Reporter, March 21, 2002.

9

WHEN TWO ELEPHANTS FIGHT IT IS THE GRASS THAT SUFFERS

The split of the TPLF (2001) and its immediate vibrations inside the labyrinth of the powerful national party, the Ethiopian People's Revolutionary Democratic Front (EPRDF), has sent tremors across the world. While the reading world public watches the event with greatcuriosity by depending on the world media's spotty coverage, the Ethiopian state and its dormant civil society suffer directly and immediately. Ethiopia is literally under siege now. Addis Ababa University, the only national university in the country, is indefinitely closed. Our knowledge-starved young minds are going to be disserved even more, because there will not be classes that would feed them. Instead, thousands are going to hang out outside the walls of the university imagining rebellion and protest and, most often, idling away around a teapot for ten, playing cards and listening to music.

Ethiopia is burning with poverty and disease. Millions are squandering their youth, their native intelligences and their fertile imaginations in poverty-drenched plastic houses and deplorable tin shacks. Millions do not any longer know the difference between the spectacularly sunny days and the dark nights. For most Ethiopians everyday life is gloomy and hopeless. All days and nights are the same. They are sick and tired of longingly eyeing the lives of the rich and famous.

They are desperate for change. Ethiopia went through so many regimes, each of which promised radical change and better times. The last regimes were the most promising, at least in the beginning. In my lifetime, the socialism of the Derg (the communist military junta that ruled Ethiopia from 1974-1987) was the first major experiment in realizing the collective will. That collective will was soon betrayed when the regime became totalitarian, when it suddenly became the enemy of the people, the very people who cast their votes to realize their life-long dream: food, shelter and clothing. They were initially given "the promised land": they woke up to a police state that randomly killed its children and their parents.

In *Notes from the Hyena's Belly*, the acclaimed Ethiopian novelist, Nega Mezlekia, gives us a perfect portrait of that oppressive regime.

The present leaders of Ethiopia came to power under the banner of dismantling a tyrannical regime that scarred the idea of socialism forever. We Ethiopians believed them. We welcomed them with open arms. They also promised a bright future, a future that would be guided by the moral imperative of treating us as humans with dignity. We were told the New Ethiopia will respect our ethnicities, languages, customs and traditions. These facets of moral personality were incorporated into the constitution. They became the pillars of living democracy and living legitimacy. Once again we hailed them. We supported their vision. We stood behind their programs.

For the last ten years, the country breezed freedom. The basic liberties of free press, freedom of thought and freedom of conscience were modestly exercised. Our prime minister spoke brilliantly and responsibly. He treated and was treated by the press freely. Many social programs aiming at developing Ethiopia were announced. Some have yet to come to fruition. For the sake of satisfying the needs of disadvantaged nationalities and ethnicities, jobs were given not necessarily to the most deserving but to those who needed them, because they had been historically excluded. Some Ethiopians did not like this scheme, but they tolerated it. Some bitterly complained. Others were anxiously waiting for the dismemberment of the regime.

The regime that stirred dreams and tickled imaginations for a considerable number of Ethiopians is now on the verge of eating itself up. The prime minster moved too hastily to fire and hire Ethiopian patriots, however tempted some of them were by the wings of desire. But democracy as a way of life is very difficult to nurture. In democratic regimes desire runs supreme. Commodities are daily temptations that desire has to fight against. Corruption is a perennial enemy of decency. Our leaders are human. Of course we have a right to expect much from them. We rightly expect them to be extraordinary. When they so fail we investigate them. If they resist we take them to the people, and discuss the issues at a public forum. If they still resist we take the extraordinary measure of constitutionally removing them from office with the consent of the people.

Democratic centralism is not enough. We need to have checks and balances with which to restrain the power of the executive, who must be checked when he overuses power, beyond the necessary and the acceptable. Democracy is not a game. It is founded on the principle that ultimately it is the people who matter. It is the people's interests and aspirations that must propel the engine of democracy. The leaders must be subservient to them, and not the other way around.

At present, the factions inside the TPLF and EPRDF have forgotten their mission, which is to serve the people. This is the pitfall of obsession with power and wealth. In democratic societies, differences are openly discussed and resolved. Surely ideological differences framing the future of the country, issues of corruption, the question of Eritrea are intrinsically important, and they ought to be aired in the open, at Parliament, through the press. They should not be enveloped in the mystical language of democratic centralism. If secrecy and intrigue are the hallmark of democratic centralism, then we the people deserve an alternative device of representation. Democratic centralism should give way to democratic decentralism. Secrecy must be replaced by the openness of dialogue free of domination and intimidation. Genuine differences must be negotiated not by silencing through tear and wear, but through argumentation along the spirited defense of discourse.

We Ethiopians were not raised in the waters of democracy. Our history is unfortunately manned by autocratic leaders and suspicious citizens. If Ethiopian culture is to flourish, we must construct democratic personalities. The democratic personality is not born. It is a work of construction. Construction is not easy. Fashioning a democratic personality is exceedingly difficult. Our leaders are advised to heed this challenge. Great leaders are not remembered through how many of their opponents they demoralized and killed. That is very easy. Once a leader kills, killing randomly becomes a habit. There is nothing heroic about that. Great is the leader who wins through persuasion, who concedes to the better argument, who swallows his pride and resigns when the people do not want him or her. Ethiopia has to create this particular kind of democratic personality.

When leaders amass too much power, when the leaders go to war to prove their virility, when leaders surrender to wealth and luxuries and deplete national resources, when worse still, they mask their weaknesses by silencing those who question them, and finally when they endanger the national agenda, it is not they who suffer, but the people, those who elected them to serve.

FROM

The Ethiopian Reporter, March 1, 2003.

10

REMEMBERING MY ETHIOPIAN BROTHERS AND SISTERS: THEY DID NOT DIE IN VAIN

The remembrance of the deaths of Ethiopian students (November, 2005) in the prime of their lives burdens my heart with anguish and sadness. Their unnecessary deaths manifest the absence of moral intelligence and conscience in those who developed the callous decision to waste lives and to squander a very precious time in modern Ethiopian history, a ripe time that could have been used to motivate youth to think positively, to spark hope and peace in their lives, so that they can think and work for their country. Clearly, our leaders thought otherwise. They brutally killed some of them. We now have tragedy on our hands. In addition to the politics of faction, we have now marked our hands with the blood of our children, the back bone of development, the measures of moral civilization. By this act, we have chosen barbarism over civilization, irrationality over rationality, death over dialogue. Indeed, this regime will be remembered for creating an Ethiopian tragedy, which will be inscribed in our memories. These heinous crimes will be confused with the many wonderful programs that this regime had so ably articulated.

The tragic death of the students compels me to rethink and relive my last ten days in Addis. I spent three of those days at the university, actively attending a conference on African Philosophy. I was there on the university compound surrounded by hundreds of students inside and outside the walls of the university. I remember how intense and unhappy the environment felt. Many students were kind enough to notice my presence among them. I could not contain myself from taking many secret looks at the youth of my homeland. Many returned my looks with gentle smiles. Some would look back with enigmatic expressions. A few would deliberately deny me the recognition that I longed for. I intuitively understood. They were unhappy with their lives, with their classes, their ragged clothes, the torn books, the tattered handbags, the tired bodies who can barely walk. Very few wore smiles on their faces. Fewer still gazed at the sky in order to protect themselves from the powerful sun that engulfed their emaciated bodies. I visited the classrooms. They are not any better than the tin shacks and plastic homes to which most of these students go when school is out, and sometimes when the dreary weekends arrive. I walked in the hallways and was chased out by corrosive sweat that would drive mosquitoes away. I entered the bathrooms and had to cover my nose and my face, so as not to be scarred by anger forever.

All is not gloom. For some, love is beautiful and good. When the university closes for vacation and on the weekends, the very few fortunate ones go home to their beautiful houses, are welcomed by their doormen and order their maids around. But those are so few not to count for very much. Most of our youth are not so fortunate to even say that they have actual homes, functional parents and normal lives. As every Ethiopian knows, many are called to our only university, and very few are chosen. The rest are forced to become hooligans, as our leaders like to call them. We now know how hooligans are constructed. It does not take much to create them. All that a nation has to do is deny them normal homes, loving parents, good schools and the right to enroll in a college. In the Ethiopian case, how many students could our national university accommodate? But look at us Ethiopians. Our ancestors fought for our survival.

They insulated us from slavery and colonialism. They left behind a few schools and a national university. Yet we are specializing in destroying it bit by bit by manning it with underpaid and highly politicized teachers. When a few daring souls question us, when they dare to think creatively and challenge our decisions, we kill them, we call them hooligans, and when we so decide we barbarously call for their untimely death. Genuine democracies are not afraid of change, most specifically they do not intimidate the very young, who learn by questioning, who are not afraid of death, but are willing to go behind the limits of experience, who teach us by introducing us to the new, the novel, the original, like some of their best counterparts in the West, where I make my living.

I could not help but compare their lives with the youth I teach in America. Marbled hallways, clean classrooms, reasonably paid teachers, sprightly students with time on their hands happily stroll on gorgeous campuses. Come weekends, they look forward to their parents' townhouses, condominiums and mansions to indulge in home cooking and summer beaches. Well rested they return to colleges and universities where they combine work with pleasure.

I remember the few students who came in to listen to my talk at the conference. They looked so hungry for knowledge, so willing to learn. But the university failed them, with its shabby classes, its unhappy teachers, sacrosanct curriculum. I remember their civility, those round Ethiopian eyes, those enigmatic smiles who speak to you. I have always hated power. For a brief moment I dreamt that I had the power to run that university efficiently so as to help these dreamy youth consummate their dreams, their hopes and their life plans.

As long as the demands of those who died are not fulfilled, those who remain behind will fight for them. My brothers and sisters did not die in vain. The moral demand will continue to burn in my heart, my grounding is with those who died.

FROM

The Ethiopian Reporter, May 2, 2001.

11

THE MEDIATIONS OF
ZARA YACOB

I would like Zara Yacob to introduce himself in his own words:

I was born in the land of the priests of Aksum. But I am
the son of a poor farmer in the district of Aksum; the
day of my birth is 25th of Nahase 1592 A.D., the third
year of the year of [King] Yaquob. By Christian baptism
I was named Zara Yacob, but people called me Warqye.
When I grew up, my father sent me to school in view
of my instruction. And after I had read the psalms of
David my teacher said to my father: "This young son
of yours is clever and has the patience to learn; if you
send him to a [higher] school, he will be a master and a
doctor." After hearing this, my father sent me to study
zema (songs). But my voice was coarse and my throat
was grating; so my school master used to laugh at me
and to tease me. I stayed there for three months, until I
overcame my sadness and went to another master who
taught *qane* (multi-meanings) and *sawsaw* (grammar).
God gave me the talent to learn faster than my com-
panions and thus compensated me for my previous
disappointment; I stayed there four years. During those
days, God as it were snatched me from the claws of
death, for as I was playing with my friends I fell into a
ravine, and I do not know how I was saved except by
a miracle from God. After I was saved I measured the
depth of the ravine with a long rope and found it to
be twenty-five fathoms and one palm [deep]. Thanking
God for saving me, I went to the house of my master.
After this I left for another school to study the interpretation of the Holy Scriptures. I remained ten years
in this type of study; I learned the interpretations of the
Frang and of our own scholars. Oftentimes their interpretation did not agree with my reason; but I withheld

> my opinion and hid in my heart all the thoughts of my mind. Having returned to my native Aksum, I taught for four years. But this period was not peaceful: for in the XIX year of King Susanyos, while afons, a Frang (Whites), was Abuna, two years [after his arrival] a great persecution spread over all Ethiopia. The king accepted the faith of the Frang, and from that time on persecuted all those who did not accept it.

The long paragraph above is a succinct and moving portrait of the Ethiopian philosopher's turbulent life. One immediately senses the presence of an independent, wise and even shrewd mind. Beyond the self-portrait, there are a few remarks about Zara Yacob by Claude Sumner[2], who is the first English-speaking scholar to introduce the thoughts of the philosopher to the philosophical world. The long debate over the authenticity of the authorship of the treatises of Zara Yacob has now been skillfully put to rest, and it is no longer doubted that Zara Yacob, and not Padre Urbino as Conti Rossini claimed, who created the literary figure of Zara Yacob.[3] It is Sumner who undertook an arduous task of comparing Zara Yacob and René Descartes on methods of thinking, for example, and has established a solid place for Zara Yacob. Indeed for Sumner, "Modern Philosophy, in the sense of a personal rationalistic critical investigation, began in Ethiopia with Zara Yacob at the same time as in England and in France."[4]

I, too, will briefly compare the two thinkers below. Most recently, the philologist V.Y. Mudimbe has also noted that Zara Yacob occupies a major place in the development of African philosophy.[5]

DESCARTES AND ZARA YACOB

To begin with, at the outset, nothing could be as stark as the differences between the material lives of these two persons. Descartes, born in 1956, a privileged European, a revered son of the Sorbonne, loftily gazed at the world from a fire place where he wondered and doubted his own existence. After a trying mental anguish, he finally arrived at the conclusion that he actually existed distinctly and clearly. *Meditations on First Philosophy* is a report on Descartes' long journey toward the belief in the existence of God. It is God, Descartes discovered during his agonizing meditations, who revealed to him the comforting and convincing proofs of his existence. More like the Greek philosophers, and unlike Descartes the modernist, Zara Yacob did not doubt his existence. He believed that he was created by God for a purpose. Zara Yacob lived in the tall and deep mountains of Ethiopia like a hunted deer, ran for his life, successfully escaped the persecution of his countrymen and finally settled into the solitary life of the mind. Like Machiavelli before him, he avoided the company of bad men, and chose to treat himself to daily conversations with God, out of which came his very brief but deep essay on the nature of knowledge, and human nature itself.

There is something however that ties these two solitary thinkers, who contributed to the unfolding of the Enlightenment. Both were ardent believers in the power of reason or intelligence as the final arbiter of human agonies. They were, each in his own way, staunch enemies of the dogmatics of the church. For both of them the light of reason should illuminate the dark regions of human thought. Neither of the two recognized teachers, priests or experts to represent the will of others by claiming to be the representatives of the will of God on earth. Finally, for Zara Yacob, God is revealed through natural reason; and for Descartes it is disclosed to intelligence.

The comparison will be incomplete, however, if one does not acknowledge the fact that Zara Yacob and Descartes believed in the power of empirical/rational proof of the elements of nature that are good for the human body, and not what the Bible supposedly revealed to Moses, Christ or Mohammed. Given his inclination, Descartes became the founder of modern philosophy of science, and Zara Yacob, in his own way, believed in common sense, a vehicle of scientific thinking in his confrontations of the dogmas of the Bible, such as the practices of fasting, marriage and sexuality.

Finally, it is crucial that one notes the following: Descartes' rationalistic modern philosophy grew out of both a secular and religious European tradition of philosophy to which he responded with his method of universal doubt. Zara Yacob on the other hand, like a lonely star, did not have a constellation of a secular tradition from which to draw. Surrounded by the powerful fortresses of religion, the philosopher had only his serene and courageous mind, ready to inspect and examine everything that he thought could not withstand the analytic presences of his relentless *Hatatas* (inquiry), which were not appreciated by a resistant and reluctant religious Ethiopian tradition, which exiled him to a cave.

I will present Zara Yacob's thoughts on three perennial topics of philosophy: (1) method of knowing God and the disclosure of truth, (2) human nature and (3) the obligations of humans.

METHOD OF KNOWING GOD

Zara Yacob's method roughly could be called a discursive subjection of faith, any faith, to a critical examination by intelligence or natural reason, which takes the form of honest searching or uncovering, called Hasasa or Hatata. Central to this project is the idea that reason itself is incomplete without God's guidance, yet reasonable human beings must subject their faith to critical self-examination before they believe. Faith in God must come after profound reasoning. All human perceptions, imaginations, judgments and apprehensions should be carefully subjected to his discursive method. Nothing should be accepted without getting tested by intelligence or natural reason. Unlike Kant, but like Descartes, faith is not superior to reason but can become superior to reason, if it is first examined and passes the test of natural reason. To put matters in perspective, consider first the way Descartes expresses what Zara Yacob is asserting, "And therefore it seems to me that I can already establish as a general principle that everything which we conceive very clearly and very distinctly is wholly true." For Descartes, distinctness and clarity are the ideals of successful communication.

Similarly for Zara Yacob, truth is clearly revealed to whoever seeks it "with the pure intelligence sat by the creator in the heart of each man." Faith then is not an irrational form of giving oneself to an unknown external power called God. Not for Zara Yacob. Faith can become a rational and reasonable activity of the mind. It is an act of the intelligence that propels thoughtful and vigilant believers, like Descartes, to believe only after activating their intelligence to demonstratively provide the necessary and sufficient conditions for believing in an overwhelming power, such as God. The proposition that "God exists" to Zara Yacob means "I have proven to myself beyond doubt that the power called God definitely exists and that I now believe, and further that from now onwards, I will not subject

God to doubt, since God has now become to me a clear object of rational faith. I now totally believe."[7]

For Zara Yacob, a style of existence such as marriage is a legitimate practice whereas monastic life is not. Marriage springs from the "law of the creator,"[8] monastic life does not. Put differently, by Zara Yacob's metaphysical yardstick, a practice such as marriage discloses a clear and distinct idea that originates in God's intention. When monastic life is measured against that yardstick, it proves to be inferior to married life. It does not pass the litmus test of reason. These claims could of course be unsettling to a nonbeliever. Even a believer may not be completely satisfied, in that one could be a devoted lover of God, and still fail to accept marriage as the only way of life. Indeed, one need not agree with Moses to disapprove of marriage. But, it is my belief that the argument in defense of marriage was not aimed at nonbelievers as much as members of the same religious convictions, most particularly at those ardent believers who consider marriage as the defilement of the body. He is challenging those "dogmatists" with the counterargument that the body was bestowed to humans not for repression or denial but for a moderate joy. The believers need not be deprived of joy. The body was given to us for a purpose, and that purpose is embodied in the constancy of marriage. That is the first implicit argument, which I just fleshed out.

The second argument was rather a commonplace in the 17th century. It is an argument that Aristotle among others initiated. That is, it takes at least two to produce an offspring, and through it populate the world. Without this act of propagation, strictly speaking, there will not be a world. Of course, Aristotle was not foolish to think that everyone will have to marry in order to have a world. In his metaphysical/biological system, some would have to produce children, and others could be celibate. Unlike Aristotle the pagan, Zara Yacob the religious thinker would not conceive of accepting children born outside the institution of marriage. To do so would be to put God on the defensive, in that in order for the children to be blessed, marriage, the law of the creator, is a necessary and sufficient condition. Otherwise marriage would have become an incoherent and indistinct norm.

Zara Yacob also has the following things to say about Mohammed, similarly, Mohammed said, "the orders I pass to you are given to me by God"; and there was no lack of writers to record miracles proving Mohammed's mission, and (people) believed in him. But we know that the teachings of Mohammed could not have come from God; those who will be born both male and female are equal in number; if we count men and women living in an area, we find as many women as men; we do not find eight or ten women for every man; for the law of creation orders one man to marry one woman. If one man marries ten women, then nine men will be without wives.[9]

According to Zara Yacob, God does not order absurdities such as "Eat this, do not eat this; today eat, tomorrow do not eat, do not eat meat today, eat it tomorrow... neither did God say to the Muslims: 'eat during the night, but do not eat during the day.'"[10] For Zara Yacob, these are unreasonable laws by human beings. God could not possibly stand behind them. These absurdities could not have emanated from human intelligence. God does not subject the human body to such traumatic deprivations. God loves his children too much to create cruel laws that disfigure the body not to say the soul. God knows the power of necessity, and the difference between necessity and luxury. As Zara Yacob put the matter, "For God created man with the same necessity for food on each day and during each month. The Jews, the Christians and the Muslims did not understand the work of God when they instituted the law of fasting; they lie when they say that God imposed fasting upon us and forbade us to eat; for our creator gave us food that we supply ourselves by it, not that we abstain from it."[11] These absurd practices are guided not by truth revealed to human intelligence but by false faith, and false faith can be recognized, if one works at it and strives to know the truth. Zara Yacob introduces a method of recognizing false faith through the following procedure.

To begin with, Zara Yacob instructs, humans are all equal in the eyes of God. This equality is expressed by the fact that God created all humans with intelligence. And because humans are fated to die, they are equal. Death does not discriminate. It is the ultimate equalizer. The human body is not entitled to immortality. Also, all persons given their intelligences, can understand God's doctrines, through revelation. These revelations constituted the moments of truth. False faith is manifestly nontruth, and cannot be revealed to persons who are fated to experience truth. Truth occurs only when all persons agree on a given matter or value; whereas it is possible for all to agree on truth, it is not possible for all to agree on falsity. Truth compels singular agreement, whereas falsity or false faith does not. For example, the fact of the existence of created things leads one to agree on a true proposition such as "Humans are created beings with a body and soul." The believer experiences the proposition as a true object of faith, whereas its opposite, "created things are because they created themselves," would not be true.

More to the point, Zara Yacob argues that the love of others is a singularly true and compelling value that all humans can agree on, whereas hate, any form of hate, cannot be elevated to a value without serious resistance coming from human reason. The second is effectively an example of a false faith that cannot pass the test of reason guided by God's doctrine. The second will be a failure of human intelligence, an abortion of reason, which is caused not by God's refusal to reveal a majestic truth that commands love, but rather humans' notorious weakness that prevents from loving deeply and unconditionally. Zara Yacob put it thus, "the Christian faith as it was founded in the days of the Gospel was not evil, since it invites all men to love one another and to practice mercy toward all, but today my countrymen have set aside the love recommended by the Gospel [and turned away toward] hatred, violence, the poison of snakes; they teach things that are vain; they do things that are evil, so the are falsely called Christians."[12] In an attempt to address the question why do humans believe in falsities, of which false faith is a particular example, he develops this proposition: God has given reason to everyone, hoping that it will be used for the search of truth, and the avoidance of falsehood. But human nature is too sluggish and weak to withstand the challenge, and this leads me to a discussion of Zara Yacob's views of human nature.

HUMAN NATURE

Human beings are exceptional beings in that—should they exercise their will power to its fullest capacity—they can decipher truth from falsehood and unfailingly choose truth over falsehood.

However, the nature of humans, when they resort to themselves only, is not sufficiently adequate to be enabling. Under their own direction, they cannot know the difference between truth and falsehood. God's direction, in the secular form of the possession of intelligence, is that power which enables individuals to judge and choose correctly. Note that the stress is less on blind faith, and more on a faith that is guided by God's reason. Humans, when unaided by God's reason, are weak—so weak that they cannot choose truth over falsehood. They get easily lured by the trappings of falsehood; wealth, status, power.

There are two kinds of laws, Zara Yacob contends: (1) the law of God, and (2) the law of humans. In order for humans to be self-governing in the realm of moral life, they must at all times consult the law of God. It is the law of God that completes the incomplete and deficient law of man. An exclusive use of (2) leads to falsehood; the use of (1) by contrast enables humans— in a fashion that (2) does not to recognize truth as truth, but truth as a semblance of falsity. It is only God who knows "the right way to act"[13] and when persons want to act rightly, they ought to consult the law of God, which is in the heart of each person. It is crucial, Zara Yacob adds, that one knows the humbling fact that everything that is of and by humans is of limited use and duration, whereas that which comes from the original source, God's doctrine as such, is illuminated by a total intelligence. Ultimately truth cannot be reached by the affairs of humans only. Humans are liars and that which comes from them is falsehood and false glory. True, the lies of humans do not affect the solid structure of the world in which they live. Lies are effective only in the defilement of human character. Thus, when we lie, it is our souls that we destroy. The world, created by the original source, remains the same. Because, "the order of God is stronger than the order of men."[14]

Humans are not merely liars. They are also are easy to tempt to errors and evil choices. It is God who sets up his children to the test of choosing evil over good. This test is God's way of separating the virtuous from the nonvirtuous. In a manner reminiscent of Aristotle's Nichomachean Ethics, he argues that it is during the various agonizing moments of choice that we reveal to the observing world who we are. Evil choices are made not because we don't know what the good is, but because we choose evil even when we know that we should not. Human nature is revealed precisely at the crucial moment of choosing. Zara Yacob is here on his own, landing upon a similar insight as Aristotle's, although there is no direct evidence that he has studied Aristotle as systematically as the Bible.

In a spiritually comforting passage, he observes that when we feel unjustly treated by God, we should not be tempted to give up our faith in him. For God has his own mystical way of judging. What one considers just when measured by human law, is unjust according to God's law. We will be rewarded for it in the other life. We live in two worlds, the material one and the spiritual one; or as Kant would have it, the phenomenal and noumenal worlds. These two worlds are governed by two different laws, and what is unjust in one is quite just in the other. As Zara Yacob put the matter, "In this world complete justice is not achieved: wicked people are in possession of the goods of this world in a satisfying degree, the humble starve; some wicked men are happy, some good men are sad, some evil men exult with joy, some righteous men weep. Therefore, after our death there must need be another life and another justice, a perfect one, in which retribution will be made to all according to their needs and those who have fulfilled the will of the creator through the light of reason and have observed the law of their nature will be rewarded."[15]

ON OBLIGATIONS

The fundamental obligation of humans is toward God. That is the first wisdom, the beginning of all knowledge. God created humans and endowed them with superior intelligence, with the hope that humans would use the endowment for the service of knowing God. As the philosopher put it, "God created us intelligent so that we may meditate on his greatness, praise him and pray to him in order to obtain the needs of our body and soul."[16] It is after we imbibe God, the symbol of reason, that we put ourselves in the condition of his willingness to be obligated toward all "others." Thus, the first foundational obligation of human beings is to love others as you would yourself, and not to do to others what you would not do to yourself. It is reason, God's gift to us, that commands us absolutely to love others as we love ourselves. Our obligations to ourselves are expressed in the secular form of meditations or the holy form of prayers.

Prayers are perhaps the deepest modalities of thinking (or if you like a fancier modernistic term of philosophizing). The Ethiopian philosophers' prayers are deeply steeped in the mastery of David's psalms. It is via these intimate prayers that the relations among human beings are illuminated; it is out of these prayers that an original mode of African philosophy is born. The persecuted philosopher, Zara Yacob, was very worried about the presence of other jealous and often vicious local religious competitors. He was intensely sensitive to the watchful eyes of the Frang with whom he was at odds. While he was self-exiled in the cave, he tells us, "I have learnt more while living alone in a cave than when I was living with scholars. What I wrote in this book is very little; but in my cave I have meditated on many other such things."[17]

Zara Yacob's breakthroughs in the world of philosophy are chiefly his few powerful pages, filled with the hermeneutic interrogation of the self via an entire surrendering to God or reason if you prefer. His meditations or prayers originated in solitude, away from the influence of derivative books. His only reference is the Bible. He meditated in a way that cannot be captured by formal language. His thoughts seemed to have been enraptured by feelings that demand a great deal of respect and attention by a resistant and arrogant modern reader. His meditations, like those of Descartes, were courageously radical. He used his intelligence to delve into the complexities, ambiguities and plenitude of the meanings of the psalms. When the psalms of David did not agree with him, no fear of authority would detain his resolute mind from striking on its own. In this medieval philosopher, we sense the presence of a fiercely independent mind.

Consider for example some of his prayers:

> Save me from the violence of men.
> Do not withhold your kindness from me.
> May your love and faithfulness constantly preserve me.
> Do not let me be disgraced.
> Turn to me and pity me.
> Guide me and lead me.
> Rescue me from my persecutors.
> Let me hear your joy and exaltation.
> Do not take away my hope.
> Give me each day what I need to satisfy the necessities of life.

Save me from the hands and tongue of men, from
bodily sickness and sorrow of the soul.

After his two years' stay in the cave, he learned that the only ever-
lasting value in the human world is the knowledge of God. Everything else is perishable, and human things are essentially vain and
contemptible, and inferior to the reason that the creator gave us, so
that we may know (a) how and what to think, (b) guide ourselves
to the knowledge of human nature and (c) finally attain profound
understanding of our obligations to ourselves and others.

His greatest prayer reads, "I am little and poor in your sight, O
Lord, make me understand what I should know about you, that I may
admire your greatness and praise you every day with a new praise."[18]

Zara Yacob has not produced the type of secondary literature
that his soulmate Descartes has. This is hardly surprising. In spite
of the seminal contributions that his short essay makes to the field
of religious thought in general, and moral philosophy in particular,
I was disheartened to discover the nonexistence of major works on
his meditations. Be that as it may, I now want to rethink his discussions of the nature of knowledge, human nature and the moral
obligations of human beings to one another.

What is truly outstanding about him is that contrary to the
domestication of the rise of the Enlightenment solely to European
cultural households and universities, here was a religious thinker,
who managed to arrive at one central motto of the Enlightenment, as Kant put it, "Have faith in your own Reason." Zara Yacob
discovered this motto of reason's legislative power from the depth
of his heart seasoned by a long and serious philosophic life in the
imposing mountains of Ethiopia. He discovered the power of his
mind to interrogate tradition, to critically examine the Gospels,
to have faith only in God, whom he accepted as the symbol of
reason, and the creator of all human beings, when he dissociated
himself from the influence of evil men, indifferent autocrats and
bad propagators of religious doctrines. He despised doctrines constructed by human beings. For him, the singularly effective doctrine is that of God: the most perfect, judicious and wise observer
of the human drama.

When he criticized doctrines, he spared no one, neither the
members of his own kind or the Frang. The African is often
portrayed by Western eyes as hopelessly irrational, impervious

to logic and reason. The Ethiopian philosopher's rational meditations conclusively disprove that. Indeed, Zara Yacob's consistent
reference to intelligence, that peculiar gift to humans, often goes
much further than the Enlightenment philosopher's similar reli-
ance on reason as the ultimate arbitrator of humankind's infamous
religious contestations. Even Kant, one of the greatest believers
in reason, dissociated reason from faith, and made God not the
symbol of reason, but rather unknowable object of faith. For Kant,
reason and faith are separable. Not so for Zara Yacob. For the
Ethiopian thinker, God is embodied in absolute reasonableness.
It was not only Hegel, who corrected Kant, when Kant separated
reason and faith. For Zara Yacob challenged the local Ethiopian
religious dogmatists as well as the European missionaries of his
time with the argument that the Gospels are to be believed in
because they are revealed by God. That is not enough. Not all the
contents of the Testaments are believable. Some are less reasonable than others. Some merely reveal the incompetence and political agendas of the prophets, including Moses and Mohammed.

As opposed to these methodological absurdities that either
project foregone conclusions, or tightly close the doors of interpretation, he pushes the open argument that every intelligent human
being has the inherent power with which to interpret the messages
of the Bible, and that nothing is to be spared from critical inter-
rogations by the mantle of reason.

For him, the rationalist, everything is subject to scrutiny and
severe test of rationality. His reflections on human nature are
equally original. He does not have many flattering things to say
to us humans, himself included. He reminds us, rather pessimisti-
cally, that we are vain, indifferent, envious and sometimes evil. As
a corrective—contrary to the English rationalist, Thomas Hobbes,
who argued that life is short, nasty and brutish, as are the human
beings who live it, and that an absolute sovereign would have to be
designated to silence men's insatiable passions for power, glory and
status—Zara Yacob instructs that it is only deep prayers and meditations that may redeem humans from their bestiality. God does not
directly speak to men when they err, he reflects; rather it is the erring
humans who must constantly inform their actions by God's guidance, and that God would listen to human agonies if he is consulted.

Political life then has much to gain from God, if it trains its citizens to habituate themselves to silent prayers in the form of medita-

tions. In the course of time, and rather invisibly, men and women might be transformed by these meditations into morally conscious citizens. Citizens who are morally/rationally formed need not be silenced and intimidated by an authoritarian or manipulative sovereign; they can be appealed to as human beings perpetually aware of the possibility of erring, of the unwanted grounding of their actions on evil. Zara Yacob places the tragic course of racial and class wars directly on the laps of human nature that is wrongly habituated to indifference, envy, vanity and self-absorbed glory.

Finally, the philosopher has quite a few challenges that he puts on human beings. The fundamental one is an absolute condemnation of ignorance as an excuse for not doing our duties. He holds men fully accountable for their actions. Similarly Zara Yacob chastises his countrymen for imputing blames of deeds that they did not follow, wars that they could have avoided, greed and selfishness that motivated their actions, and the persecutions of all those whom they disgraced with their ways and doctrines.

For him, all these terrible actions are manifestly tragic exemplifications of the essence of a moral vision guided by the fear of God. Humans are simply fearful of what they should not fear, for example death; and fearless of precisely those dreadful predilections that lure individuals to do the socially disgraceful: status, glory, fame and wealth.

The philosopher preaches that moderation and self-control are the cardinal virtues that a medieval Ethiopia and, through it, the selfish and cruel world desperately needs. And, from what we know about the way he lived, he himself was a model of a moral hero, an ethical man, born to an unethical milieu. Finally, Zara Yacob makes great moral strides in the solution of a major problem in moral philosophy, namely when various individuals' images of God produce hostile doctrines that are eminently opposed to each other, what is to be done to avert cruel civil wars? His answers are challenging. First, for him, there is only one incontestable doctrine, as far as the believers are concerned. He calls it God's doctrine, which he sharply distinguishes from men's doctrine. God's doctrine is motivated by the search for truth, whereas human doctrine is tempted by falsehoods cloaked as truth. If one follows God's doctrine, one is invariably led to experience the disclosure of truth, through which one can develop appropriate sense of duties, of obligations to oneself and all those others with whom we share the world.

Through numerous reflections on methods of knowing, on human nature, and finally on the scope of moral obligations, each of which are guided by comprehensive reason filled with moral sensibilities, this solitary Ethiopian thinker, who lived in a cave for two years, managed to contribute to the founding of what I wish to call African Enlightenment in the 17th century.

It is he who indigenized reason, and simultaneously gave it a regional and international color, for which his modern readers ought to be enormously grateful. Zara Yacob's indiginization of philosophy as a religious thinker was not flawless, however. Consistent with the dominant prejudices of the age, his views of non-Christians, particularly Jews and Muslims, were not positive.[19] Indeed, his strong belief in the power of reason did not lead him to develop a politically fair principle of toleration. Similarly, his insistence, like Aristotle before him, that marriage is part of the ontology of being would be shaken by tough challenges from feminists and postmodernists of the contemporary milieu. If we evaluate his program by the yardsticks of modernity, there is much in his vision of the good life that many persons would find quite oppressive and very intolerant. But still, in contemporary hermeneutics of discussions of reading the Bible, there is no substitute to the type of confidence and independence of mind, needed for interpretation, which Zara Yacob's philosophy solidly established.

NOTES

1. I would like to thank Professors Glenn Tinder and Winston Langley of the University of Massachusetts for reading this paper and commenting on it. I would like to thank as well Professor Edouard Bustan for providing me with a forum at the African Studies Center of Boston University to discuss my paper. Finally, my greatest thanks to May Farhat of Harvard University for her invaluable comments.

2. Claude, Sumner, "The Treatise of Zara Yaquob," in *Ethiopian Philosophy*, Vol. II (Addis Ababa: Commercial Printing Press, 1976), p.

3. Ibid., ff. See as well the summary of the debate in Claude Sumner, *The Source of African Philosophy: The Ethiopian Philosophy of Man* (Stuttgart: Franz Steiner Verlag, 1986), pp. 41-42.

4. Sumner, *The Source of African Philosophy*, p. 42.

5. V. Y. Mudimbe, *The Invention of Africa* (Bloomington: Indiana University Press, 1988).

6. René Descartes, *Meditations* (New York: The Bobbs-Merrill Company, 1960), p. 34.

7. Zara Yacob, *Meditations*, p. 9.

8. Ibid.

9. Ibid., p. 10.

10. Ibid., p. 11.

11. Ibid. For a remarkably similar argument but without explicit religious bent, see Aristotle's *The Nicomachean Ethics* (Cambridge, MA: Harvard University Press, 1982). See the discussions of Moral Evil in Book iii.

12. Zara Yacob, p. 13.

13. Ibid.

14. Ibid.

15. Ibid., p. 14.

16. Ibid., p. 16.

17. Ibid., p. 17.

18. Ibid., p. 19.

19. Zara Yacob does not directly mention Christ himself, but is severe in his criticism of the European and Ethiopian Christians of his time, as is clearly stated in various passages such as the following, "the Frang tell us; 'God's doctrine is not with you, but with us'" (p. 12) and "However, to say the truth, the Christian faith as was founded in the days of the Gospel was not evil, since it invites all men to love one another and to practice mercy towards all. But today my countrymen have set aside the love recommended by the Gospel (and turned away towards) hatred, violence" (pp., 12-13). Zara Yacob would have few disagreements with the interpretations of Christianity in the able hands of the distinguished political philosopher, Glenn Tinder. In his highly acclaimed book, *The Political Meaning of Christianity* (New York: Harper Collins Paperback Edition, 1991), Professor Tinder has introduced the notion that Christianity is guided by the vision of the prophetic Stance, which is based "on two basic Christian tenets, the selfish nature of humans and the hope that is present in Christ" (p. 13).

FROM

East African Forum, September 10, 2000.

12

RENDEZVOUS WITH VICTORY: CELEBRATING OUR ETHIOPIAN SPORTS HEROES

At the November 4, 2001, New York Marathon, Tesfaye Jifar, a 25-year-old Ethiopian who had never before won a marathon and who runs half-blind because he lost his right eye to a bull's horn in his youth, set a new course record. Jifar's victory, like those of other Ethiopian runners who have dominated marathons in recent years, helps to heal the wounded pride of a nation.

For the past several years, the world has been reluctantly treated to the usual media-driven scenes of Ethiopian pain: savage war, terrorized civilians everywhere, big-eyed hungry Ethiopian children.

But joy and pride in accomplishment meet whenever Ethiopian athletes dominate the world stage, as they did in New York and at the 2000 Sydney Olympics. The mighty Ethiopia rises again. At Sydney, the beautifully lithe bodies of Haile, Abera, Mezgebu, Derartu and Tola emerged on the vast tracks to the applause of the observing world. Thin and sinewy arms, unimposing muscles, slender but mightily strong legs, determined faces, they run to victory: steadily, cautiously and intelligently.

I remember how nervous I was when Abera and Tola maintained that quiet and constant rhythm for over 20 miles, unbothered by the powerful Kenyan runner ahead of them, giving the impression to the inexperienced observer that they might not win.

The world knows Ethiopia for emaciated bodies, barbaric warmongers, perennial hosts of famine. We have always reminded the world of our pain, as if we had chosen it, as if we have the power of overcoming the wings of nature. While singled out as an example of fiasco, or tragedy, Ethiopia has emerged as the land of marathoners.

Our runners recover our tarnished history. They do not relent. They welcome victory calmly, quietly, graciously and humbly, the classical attributes of the Ethiopian soul. Our runners, you must know, model themselves after that perfect marathoner, Abebe Bikila. They appropriate Bikila's classical blend of sheer stamina with controlled focus informed by a religious vision, and make it their own.

Geneticists beware! Do not ascribe these victories to special genes. It is hard work on the steep highlands of East Africa that produced these powerful legs that seem to run forever. And it is the hard history of our country that enables our victory to shine so brightly.

FROM

Africana.com, September 20, 2000.

1 3

TWO CONCEPTS OF ETHNICITY

The recent explosion of the politics of ethnicity in modern Ethiopia calls for a retheorizing of the idea of ethnicity itself. The situation is so grave that it compels a philosophical intervention. I would like to argue that ethnicity could be viewed as positive and negative, which I would call positive ethnicity (PE) and negative ethnicity (NE). We need to salvage the positive merits of ethnicity, and avoid the strong temptation of divesting individuals and groups of the psychological and historically necessary need of investing in ethnicity as a way of defending the differences that mean so much to those who believe in them. The unnecessary contamination of ethnicity need not force us to throw out the baby with the bathwater.

The essential core of PE is the idea of diversity. The attributes of diversity are distinctness of experience expressed in language, customs, traditions and ways of seeing and doing things; individuality; dissimilarity of experience; constructive articulations of unique ways of experiencing the world; and openness.

NE, as most people readily and conveniently understand it, holds the core ideas of blood and kinship, and the attributes of these core ideas are the naturalization of customs and traditions as peculiar to an ethnic group; the forging of alliances and interests on the presumed existence of a group that shares those interests and passions; the similarity of experience; destructive articulations of ways of seeing, knowing and doing things; aversion of differences; denial of the formation of factions between groups perceived to be divergent; and finally and most negatively, bolstering and systematically defending closedness as a tool of argumentation.

In his well-reasoned article in the *Addis Tribune* (October 4, 2004) Dr. Messay Kebede has quite convincingly articulated the political dangers of NE, particularly when unanimity becomes the sole criterion by which groups of people are put in a single basket, as if there are no individuals who would like to reserve the right of choosing the baskets in which they would like to be. The obsession with NE denies existentially serious individuals the right to choose, the crucial right to be. Instead individuals are coerced to force themselves inside uncomfortable boxes of political inconvenience, the language of ethnic bureaucrats.

Diversity has been a virtue worth defending for millennia. A generation of philosophers has linked diversity with the foundational virtue of freedom. The flourishing of an individual is dependent on how free they feel to express their diverse desires. The nature to express diverse desires or how free we feel to express them is a true facet of personality only when one looks at human history naturally, as if we are not historical beings, born to a specific space, at a specific time, to a particular region of the world. In this special sense, humans are geographical beings. As children of time, space and geography, in the course of living their lives they develop ethnicity, which is an aspect of cultural diversity. As ethnic beings with diverse desires, they further develop distinct ways of knowing, seeing, and doing that are exemplified as customs and traditions. Ethnicity in this sense is extrapolated from the ethos that history and geography saddle our fragile existence.

It is not only groups who are diverse, as we have been socialized to think. Groups that are diverse are groups with individual distinctions of desire. Within groups, there are further individual distinctions of desire, of passion, of individual culture, albeit implicitly. For the sake of fitting in, we suppress the yearning for freedom, the passion for life. Very few of us think of diversity in this deep and sensible way. However, unconsciously, all of us suppress this desire to be free from our attachment to our ethnicity, even when it is the cement of ethnicity that never fulfills us, that never leads us to happiness. PE, as an authentic love of ethnicity, does not have to suppress the individual Eros for life.

An erotic relationship with our life, as existentially serious, ought to allow us to grow as genuine individuals with specific rights, the rights that safeguard us to be open to others and for others to be open to us. Openness gradually becomes a way of life, an ethics of living within the ethnic glue and toward those who are not part of our ethnic group. By using ourselves as measures of happiness and freedom-acting, we can eventually learn to understand the needs of those outside the circle of blood and kinship. These self-imposed relations are profoundly complicating relationships among the Oromos, Tigreans and Amharas in modern Ethiopia. The ethnic makeup of our leaders is not helping matters either.

Doing what makes you happy and free will ultimately lead to make others feel the same way. Developing empathy for your fellow man, whoever he may be, you cannot help but open up to him. Once we develop this open disposition, we can comfortably accommodate other human beings not as the "other" but as a human being made out of the same fabric, but who seems an other only because history and geography have determined the different ways of seeing and being. Difference itself becomes a historical product that can be accommodated by love and understanding.

The accommodation of difference does not require the death of the individual. The recognition of difference requires of us to emerge out of the cocoon of dealing with those who are like us. That is easy. Genuine recognition begins with the modest assumption that no other human being is outside the region of our understanding if we sincerely try. The catastrophes of the holocaust, ethnic cleansing in Rwanda and, closer to our home, the ongoing ethnic conflicts in Ethiopia are caused less by the impenetrability of the other, and more directly by the overwhelming saturation of our modern consciousness with the negative form of ethnicity, that sometimes blends itself with philistine nationalism.

NE contaminates the current reality in Ethiopia to a degree that has hopelessly offended some of the minority ethnic groups, such as the Amharas that are not in power now, but were power holders not very long ago. Dr. Kebede is quite right when he astutely observes that "previous Ethiopian regimes had ruled Ethiopia in the name of Amhara people while maintaining the people in a abject condition of poverty and silence, so too the new leaders rule Ethiopia for Tigray while shutting up and dislocating its people" (*Addis Tribune*, October 19, 2001, p. 8). This example is a classic illustration of the crass form of NE. There are more such appalling examples.

To hide real issues that continue to affect the lives of millions of Ethiopians, our leaders manipulate blood and kinship ties. Through these insidious tactics of NE, the Ethiopian masses are deliberately kept ignorant. Democracy is centralized precisely because ethnic leaders do not want them to see through it, to go behind the veil and unmask the machinations of power and intrigue. The willing members of these ethnic groups among the most numerous, the Oromos, and among the numerical minorities, the Tigreans, are bamboozled by the myths of history and are defined by degenerate forms of difference that convince them that their needs, desires and passions can only be represented by their blood brothers and kin.

All that one has to do is roam the tin houses and plastic shelters of Addis where millions fester to realize the hollowness of the claim. If a blood member of these ethnicities dares to point out the miserable reality, she is hounded by the blood leaders, and silenced by intimidation, and when absolutely necessary is brutally killed, in the name of an atrocious ethnic solidarity, the backwaters of the abuse of ethnicity. African political reality is marred by this deliberate misuse of ethnicity as NE.

If ordinary Ethiopian peasants, workers, civil servants and many others are encouraged to think for themselves, divisive ethnic leaders will be stunned by the emergence of independent thinking far removed from the coercive frames and fences of negative ethnicity. PE provides a potent dosage of the desperately needed virtues of authentic individuality, dissimilarity of experience, difference and distinct ways of experiencing the world. The peoples' economic needs, their passions, their aspirations and plans for their children's future will be guided by rationality and compassion consecrated in the formation of smart alliances. Again PE provides the necessary cushion. The stagnant and shameful Ethiopian economic geography that has been dormant for centuries will begin to change precisely because the people will have discovered how to use ethnicity positively. When PE is used shrewdly the Oromo peasant and worker will immediately sense that there is a commonality of suffering and shattered dreams that ties with his Amhara peasants and workers, and with his Tigrean peasants and workers, and that in the end it is the most upright and morally and technically intelligent leader that she must choose. A leader will be chosen not because he is an Amhara or Oromo. His leadership qualifications and his moral makeup impose themselves on the voters.

Once again Kebede is right, when he wisely advises that "We Ethiopians must learn that when it comes to politics, it is better to trust aliens than kin, just as we must understand that sane politics is a game resulting in everybody becoming a winner. The main requirement for instituting this kind of game is the use of Pan-Ethiopian standards" (p. 4). Wise indeed. We all remember how Ethiopian autocratic emperors and self-acknowledged tyrannical communists used NE to entrench their heels in the Ethiopian political soil, but times change, new sensibilities emerge, consciousness gets transformed. Our leaders should positively exploit these positive developments by engaging PE.

The current leaders, Meles Zenawi chief among them, have a chance to leave a constructive legacy behind. When Ethiopia was at war with Eritrea, in a series of articles in *Walta Information Center* (1995), I modestly advised the prime minister to forge a new Ethiopia, a genuinely democratic Ethiopia led by a prime minister who presents himself as an Ethiopian, without ever apologizing for his ethnic roots, but cherish them as the voices of genuine diversity, individuality, healthy distinctness, which are precisely the emblems of universal rights of particular ethnic groups.

I advise the president again to use his hard-earned Ethiopian nationality and international fame as a new breed of African leader to delink his name from the tragedy at Addis Ababa University, as I pointed out in "Remembering My Ethiopian Brothers and Sisters" (essay no. 36), and spend his remaining days to leave a positive image of his regime, and rejuvenate its promising beginnings. It is for these laudable purposes that the banner of positive ethnicity could be constructively used.

Narrow-mindedness of whatever form is a vice that must be combated as Frantz Fanon, the acclaimed author of *The Wretched of the Earth*, taught us by national consciousness. National consciousness, when fully realized, transcends both PE and NE. PE in particular becomes redundant, once the idea of the nation replaces the notion of ethnicity. National consciousness displaces ethnic consciousness, at the minimum; it stifles the otherwise inevitable degeneration of PE into NE. Ethnicity can be effectively utilized to inform the bases of new democratic sensibilities. All Ethiopians can be taught to admire our differences as members of historically generated ethnic groups and as thinking beings, as beings born with the "capacity to think." We can be retaught to trust more and not less, to expunge from the fibers of our being the poison of suspicion and forced unanimity. We Ethiopians should learn how not to hide behind artificial pluralism, a pluralism that does not allow us to freely and courageously criticize our leaders when they make shameful mistakes in our name. As beings with the capacity to think, we must use this power to peacefully challenge our leaders when they fail to carry out the tasks that we mandated them to perform. The Ethiopian people should not be used as pawns, which we consult only when we are in trouble. That is treason. It is immoral and politically suicidal. They should consult us, appeal to us, inform us, when they are not in crises. And the people should know the difference between genuine consultation and manipulative appeal.

The nationalism and internationalism of Meles should not be used destructively, as the dissenters, perhaps, correctly allege. Power need not be uses as Bonapartism, as Meles shrewdly alleges is the way that the dissidents are using it. One could convincingly argue that Bonapartism is double pronged. But these attacks and counter attacks are useless in the end as I recently argued in "When Two Elephants Fight It Is the Grass That Suffers" (essay no. 35).

Meles should forge a new Ethiopia blessed by the beauty and diversity of a multiethnic state.

FROM

Addis Tribune, August 30, 2002.

14

ZARA YACOB, 17TH CENTURY RATIONALIST: ON THE RATIONALITY OF THE HEART

Zara Yacob, the subject of my book *Zara Yacob: Rationality of the Human Heart*, lived in the 17th century in Ethiopia, and is the founder of rationality in Africa (see essay no. 37). He was a contemporary of René Descartes, the founder of rationality in France. He was born at a time in which Europe was looking for adventures and explorations of the world. During this time Ethiopia, the birthplace of Christianity, had captured the imaginations of the Portuguese Jesuits, who attempted to spread Catholicism, and managed to briefly convert Ethiopian King Susyenonos. This act repulsed Zara Yacob, partly because he disagreed with the preaching of the Jesuit teachers, and partly because he wanted to defend Ethiopia's sovereignty. It is at this juncture that he develops an original notion of rationality in his *Treatise*, which he called conversations with the transcendent, out of which I will attempt to develop his vision of the "rationality of the heart."

ZARA YACOB'S VISION OF THE RATIONALITY OF THE HEART

His method of philosophizing is that of a novelist. Marguerite Duras' method of novelizing, as displayed in her last major work, *C'est tout*, comes to mind. In this extraordinary novel, she creates another, in the form of a lover, whom she calls Yann, and with whom she shares her meditations on love and death. Similarly, Zara Yacob creates a powerful and perfect other, whom he calls God, and to whom he speaks every day. Prayerful discourses are the content of this conversation, during which he searches for this God. He looks for him through Hasasa (meditating). God maintains this relationship with Zara Yacob through revealing and hiding. The philosopher celebrates the revealing in the form of thankful prayers. He patiently waits for God, when he is hidden from him through intense prayers of longing and loving anxiety. His belief in God belongs to a form of belief that cannot be disconfirmed. This form of belief is a necessary analytic truth, and not a contingent one.

At the center of Zara Yacob's originality lies the hitherto unrecognized place of the human heart in philosophical activity. No philosopher before or after him (Blaise Pascal, the writer, excepted) had attached such a firm significance to the function of the human heart. Philosophers before and after him tend to ignore the role of the human heart in thinking, or they sharply distinguish the heart from the mind, and treat the mind as the seat of thinking, and the heart as the organ of feeling. For Zara Yacob reason itself is placed in the heart, and not in the brain. It is as if the mind itself is located in the heart, and not outside it.

In classical phrases, he tells us "To the person who seeks it, truth is immediately revealed. Indeed he who investigates with the pure intelligence set by the creator in the heart of each man and scrutinizes the order and laws of creation will discover the truth" (*Zara Yacob*, A lecture at Emmerson College, ON Feb 22, 2001). It is the creator who placed intelligence or the ability to reason in the human heart. He is arguing that what we call analytical thinking is itself a function of the heart, and that the heart has been incorrectly described as the organ that processes feelings only. Zara Yacob contends that thinking itself is the activity of the heart, and that genuine thinking is passionate, and passion as an expression of feeling is an integral part of thought. Thought is a passion for truth. The passion for truth takes place inside our hearts, before it is communicated through language. Speaking truth or searching for it or meditating about it, is sown in the heart. Truth germinates there, and then it explodes in the form of the passion of speech. Our intelligence tells us to do the right things. God withdraws from our everyday lives once he implants intelligence in our hearts. But He dwells in our actions. He has given us the power with which to live the appropriate life of reason. This reasonable God is always available for direction but only when we consult him through Hasasa (meditation) and Hatata (searching). He gently directs us through examples, not through harsh commandments. He does not tell us what to do. He shows us what we can do, if we use our heart's intelligence correctly.

However, years of scientific scholarship have treated the human heart as particularly suited to absorb and process delicate emotional information. The heart has been so stereotyped that we rarely think of it as a center of reliable and carefully thought out information. When one wants to belittle another persons' thought we are known to say, "your heart is in the right place," meaning that you are not thinking well, if you were, you would not think that way. Zara Yacob reverses this kind of talk. The intelligently created being thinks in and through the heart. This point, Zara Yacob's very own, is repeatedly underscored in the *Treatise*.

Rationality for Zara Yacob is an activity of the human heart blessed by a moral intelligence that is given to all human beings, should they choose to make use of this extraordinary gift. Having a gift and actually using it are of course two different activities. But for those who would like to do the morally right thing, the heart is ready to help them do the task, the important task of performing in a morally worthy manner. Such individuals do not have to go beyond consulting their heart when they agonize over their decisions, over their choices and over their dreams of seeking to be exceptional human beings. In almost every other page of the *Treatise*, both Zara Yacob and Walda Heywat (Zara Yacob's student and successor) continue to refer to the human heart as the ultimate place of profound thought. In none of the modalities of rationality is the human heart acknowledged as the source of thought. The heart is subtly treated as the place of meandering emotions and fickle feelings, or else it is simply ignored. Zara Yacob was the first to reconfigure rationality, by reordering the relationship between the brain and the heart. The brain for him is a processing machine, nothing more beyond that. The heart is the home of thought. The brain's function is not the production of thought, as the rationality of Descartes assumed. The production of thought is an activity of the heart.

The children of modernity and advocates of scientific rationality attempt to ground rationality in tradition and customs. Zara Yacob seeks to free rationality from tradition, and locality. For him there is a universal God who created all human beings as equal.

All of us are made of the same fabric. Although we do not speak the same language, all of us are capable of extending our moral imagination to understand the needs and passions of the so-called others. There is no need for techniques of understanding "others," as if they are made of a different fabric. It does not require much to understand the languages of despair and hunger. All that we need to do is decide how the hungry must be feeling, and what our duties are to end that condition, particularly when we are sitting on wealth and power that we do not really need, apart from the status and power that accompany that condition, and how it sometimes blinds our vision, and crowds our ears with flattery and praise. None of this requires transversality to understand. We are already in possession of intelligence by which we can identify our duties and obligations. All that we need to do is wake up the sluggish self.

What we should fear the most is the other in us: the vain, selfish and self-regarding other. The "other" outside will be taken care of by the just transcendent. The frightening other is us, when we become overwhelmed by our projects, our plans, our careers, at the expense of all those individuals who can benefit from our attention, our kindness and care. However difficult the challenging task is, the death of the morally unmotivated other, is the death of the other in us. That other needs to be cured from it, and be replaced by a vigilant, morally attentive, caring other, who listens to the voice of the heart. The cultivation of the moral self is one of the perennial themes of moral philosophy. For millennia some philosophers have attempted to cultivate a moral citizen. Others, the philosopher Thomas Hobbes chief among them, have argued that there is no such self. The real self is selfish and brutish, whose vices only the law can silence. Zara Yacob also does not have much regard for the natural self, and yet he thinks that this selfish self can be cured by the rationality of the heart, if it dutifully prays to the transcendent. The decision to have a prayerful attitude toward life is the beginning of the healing process. Without that initial decision nothing can be accomplished. The broken self of modernity suffers from this unprayerful attitude, this thankless thinking. The rationality of the heart can enable the broken self to mend its heart.

IN DEFENSE OF THE RATIONALITY OF THE HEART

The rationality of the heart attempts to solve human problems through the mediation of the heart, the heart as the dwelling place of thought; and I am enormously grateful to Zara Yacob for leaving such a powerful vehicle of thought that I am convinced would be in service of modernity, because modernity is desperately in need of the language of the heart. One way of celebrating the virtues, not to say the distinctiveness, of the rationality of the heart (RH) is to compare it to scientific rationality (SR). I will begin with a detailed discussion of SR, and then proceed to contrast it with RH.

SR is the dominant form of thought in the Western world, and the non-Western world seems to be rapidly racing to embrace it. Before proceeding to compare these rationalities, I would first like to clearly articulate the nature of SR. For the most part SR is exclusively focused on meeting the economical and psychological needs of the individual. On this view rational is the individual who articulates his individual needs and then devises the appropriate means with which to satisfy them. The articulated ends must fit the chosen means perfectly; otherwise the action is irrational. Moreover, the rational individual is not expected to take the needs of others into account, unless recognizing and satisfying their needs is crucial for the satisfaction of their own life plan.

Modernity in Africa is being rapidly rationalized, but I think this decision is a mistaken one. To be sure, the rich and powerful are using SR for their own ends. Some of the richest men in the world are now in Africa: shamelessly depleting African resources; enriching themselves on the backs of the poor; subjecting six-year-olds to psychological and physical abuse; sending their children to the most expensive universities in the West; when they can they place their own children in unearned positions of power and financial comfort. Merit is a plaything of the scientific rationalists, indifference to suffering is a way of life, the struggle of the fittest is an ideology, going to church and praying is a habit without the heart. The church in Africa is the rich man's church. It is there to justify the begetting of wealth by any means necessary, since the rich and powerful believe that God helps only those who can help themselves. It is widely believed that the poor are poor because they cannot help themselves, that they are irrational, that they do not plan well. These are the myths of SR that have been used as weapons of the rich.

RH has the potential to redeem us all from ourselves, from the slumber of our sleep, our callousness and indifference. These are turbulent times. Indifference is the signifier of the age. Game playing is the name of human relations. We play people. We like to say "play him this way." "Make sure that you play her that way" is the other side of the coin. We do this without shame. We even like to say (sadly), "do not be emotional, be reasonable." Note the way we separate emotion from reason. Worse still, we always make sure that our decisions are rational, to the extent that we remove our passions, the center of emotion from guiding our decisions. Just imagine the persons that we encounter daily; those who devotedly clean our offices, those who silently man our elevators, those who look after our children when we work away long hours, those who smilingly serve us at restaurants. We treat them indifferently. We say to ourselves they are doing their job, performing a task for which they are being paid. Yet, we know that most of these jobs are inadequately paid, are miserable and insulting. They deaden the nerves. They harden and embitter the people who perform them. Study after study has documented this.

To respond to these facts of modern life requires not only the calculative services of SR but also more fundamentally the participation of the human heart, and that is how RH enters the picture, to protect us against ourselves. When we listen to the heart—the seat of thought—we will not suffer from the subtle assaults of thoughtlessness in the peculiar form of indifference and internalized cruelty. We have become accustomed not to respond to these conditions, as Zara Yacob and Walda Heywat demand from our hearts. We conclude too quickly that these individuals are fated to live this way, and that the best that SR enables us to do for them is at least employ them. Even that is not looked at as a right that these human beings have.

Indifference and cruelty, we have been told by a long line of philosophers (Plato, Aristotle, Kant and Hobbes) and novelists (Dostoyevsky and Camus), are natural emotions, and there is very little that we can do to change them. The philosophers and novelists seem to be right if we evaluate the proposition by the yardstick of human practices over a long period of human history. A proposition is not only a descriptive affirmation of a practice, but also a symbol, however mythical the symbol, is of possibility and a new way of leading our lives against the background of what we know about human beings. The symbolic possibility challenges human beings by signaling to them that they can be other than what they have become.

Nothing can c
that there is very li
constantly bombard
condition. SR does
is the exact calculati
ment to come out
decide to pay attent
flooded with the wa
fellow human being
those who labor sil
tion with the garag
in our heart for th
our daily moral pra
sometimes preache
we are thinking thr
enforcing the prin
bureaucrats.

This is not to say that principles are not important. They are so important that the heart itself can produce them. Principles do not have a life of their own. To think is not merely to be stimulated by moral reason. Thinking is to be genuinely affected by pain in the world. It is an exercise in going out of the enclosed space of self-obsession to embrace another human being. To think is not merely to be stimulated by moral reason. Thinking is genuinely affected by pain in the world. It is an exercise in going out of the enclosed space of self-obsession to embrace another human being. Thinking in this sense is an activity of the heart. To argue that the call to action that the thinking heart stimulates is rational is not to denigrate the role of moral principles. In a very subtle sense the principles of reason are not produced by the mind but are generated by the activity of the heart. Principles are the vehicles of the thought that takes place in the heart itself, and which the brain organizes. Principles are the mediations of thought. This is particularly true of moral thought, which is the sphere to which I am applying RH, provoked by Zara Yacob's orginal modernity anchored on the rationality of the heart.

FROM

The Communicator, April 27, 2001

SOURCES

T. Kiros, *Zara Yacob: On the Rationality of the Human Heart*, Trenton, New Jersey: The Red Sea Press, 2005.

Zara Yacob, *The Treatise of Zara Yacob and of Walda Heywot: Text and Authorsip by Claude Sumner (1976-1978)*, Addis Ababa University Press, Addis, Ethiopia.

Margaret Duras, *C'est Tout*, Seven Stories Press: US, 1998.

15

INTELLECTUALS AND RADICAL DEMOCRACY

There is nothing special about intellectuals. The term "intellectual" simply denotes someone who is fascinated with ideas. Sometime the ideas are clear, purposeful and meaningful. Sometimes they are not. When they are not so meaningful, the intellectual remains fascinated with them, for their own sake, very much like the artist who does art for art's sake.

By this definition, then, anybody who is fascinated with ideas is an intellectual. But there are wrinkles to the definition. The intellectual is further distinguished from the ordinary person who gets fascinated by ideas because the intellectual strides a further step and separates himself from the average person by elevating his ideas into esoteric specialties, so that he could claim that only he has the appropriate tools with which to decipher those difficult ideas.

Thus some intellectuals specialize in the natural sciences. Others excel in the humanity broadly understood. Many develop expertise in the social sciences. During this crucial time of the transformation of knowledge from common sense to the modern disciplines, the ordinary intellectual and his fascination with ideas is left behind. The knowers are separated from the non-knowers.

Surely, the members of the current regime in Ethiopia have sacrificed body and soul to liberate Ethiopia from the Derg. Ethiopians remain grateful for that. While fighting for seventeen years in the rugged plateaus of Ethiopia, they have developed expertise in the art of war. They fought heroically to give us a new and, in the beginning, a radically democratic regime. Many Ethiopians fondly remember their arrival on the Ethiopian scene. Ethiopians from all walks of life stretched their arms to welcome them. Many began to dream again. Many have deferred their dreams since.

One can say that the leaders' fascination with the art of war qualifies them as intellectuals in their own right. The defense of the country and the appropriate knowledge of that is their domain. This knowledge has rightly qualified some of them for leadership positions. That is appropriate. But that qualification is radically different from the qualifications needed to run a country by attending to the nation's multifaceted needs, in the complex era of globalization. There are underused and extremely able intellectuals who should fill those positions.

Administering Ethiopia is different from defending it. The administration of Ethiopia, in contrast to defending it, belongs to the domain of intellectuals and their ever-complex specialties. The desiderata for these positions call for different criteria. The criteria should be merit combined with integrity. Again, Ethiopia is blessed with an impressive availability of a highly qualified intelligentsia rightly fascinated with highly technical disciplines ranging from economists to natural scientists.

Most of our leaders unfortunately do not have the requisite knowledge to man our huge bureaucracy, for a fault not their own. Most were busy defending the country, as masters of the art of war, no easy undertaking. The services of this sleepy intelligentsia could be solicited through an annual conference that the prime minster could convene, at which experts in all fields could present their ideas without fear. They could forward programs about where Ethiopia should go. The prime minister could use these occasions to learn and not compete with those who really know, unless their ideas are unfeasible or irrelevant—then the prime minister and his advisors could present their objections through the force of the better argument, free of domination. Establishing such a public forum is one of the central pillars of radical democracy. Indeed, it is the most important value that genuine democracies celebrate. Modern Ethiopia too needs this precious value.

FROM

The Ethiopian Reporter, April 5, 2002.

16

JUSTICE

In "What Is a Future Life?" (*Dekialula*, March 7, 2006), I wrote:

> A future life is a chance to live the good life, or at least, the acceptable life. This possibility of a good life can be secured only if the self is guaranteed a consistent access to the internal needs of the body. There is no self without these internal needs. Surely these are not the only needs of the self. But these needs are necessary conditions for the future of the self, including the future cultivation of other needs, other than the internal needs of the body.
>
> Where these internal needs are absent, however, there is (a) no future, (b) no life chance and (c) no future with meaningful life chance. (A), (b) and (c) are anchored on the availabilities of fundamental goods. The fundamental needs are food, shelter, clothing and health.
>
> Put syllogistically, the argument is this: The human self needs fundamental goods to maintain its selfhood famished bodies are deprived of these goods. African bodies are therefore denied of a future with life chances.

Justice, a cardinal principle of Maat[1], ought to address the deplorable conditions of injustice manifest in a scene that I described in *Dekialula*, "Waiting for Change," November, 28, 2007:

> Pain. Death. Tears. Cries. Rocks and stones. Desperate mothers parting from their dead sons and daughters; priests chanting peace; the young impatiently throwing rocks and stones; the police responding with excessive force; leaders commanding away from the comfort of the palace; the rich and powerful dancing at the Sheraton; the desperate and alienated sharing a pot of tea and whisking away flies in tea shops; sexual

diseases spreading in the shantytowns inside dark tin houses, these scenes are the features of contemporary Ethiopian lives. These scenes were the marks of primitive regimes in prepolitical times. Contemporary Ethiopia is indeed moving backwards towards a prepolitical era.

Armored with Maat, and most profoundly mediated by justice, African future leaders, extracted from the citizenry, ought to internalize justice as a living feature of their hearts as they address the perennial needs of the citizens. On this level, justice can be articulated in several ways. I modestly suggest two modes:

1. Justice could be worked out textually by a writer/thinker. An example of the first is the world-famous Plato, author of *The Republic*, who gave us a vision of a just polis; and in our time, John Rawls, the American philosopher, gave us his theory of justice. These two are examples of justice from the top.

2. There is a mode of addressing justice as propelled by the heart. This mode takes place on the streets of the polis, where thousands and millions of people, should they so want, flood the streets, until after justice is served, and the pangs of hunger, the perenniality of poverty, deplorable inequalities and the deaths of protestors are protested against, and people remain on the streets, facing death, until their demands are met by the powers to be. This is an example of justice from below, from the trenches.

Change under the tutelage of a just leader, or better still organized by a social movement, must be tenacious, resolute and populated by numbers. Consider the following example. In the Ethiopian condition, millions of people live in tin houses, millions go without food and clothing and yet 1% of the population dances away the evenings and eats away at fancy hotels. By the standards of Maat's comportment, this prepolitical condition is so unacceptable that it must be protested against by the people in revolt. The just way of responding to this condition is marching in the streets in the millions and refusing to leave the space of revolt, unless a policy of transferring wealth from those who have it in excess to those who have nothing is readily enacted. Justice must be put on the march, lead by just leaders of the people. A functional state led by a leader with the organizing principle of justice must attend to the demands of the people and change their condition.

From

Dekialula, March 5, 2006

NOTE

1. In ancient Egypt, Maat was the personification of the fundamental order of the universe without which all of creation would perish. The primary duty of the pharaoh was to uphold this order by maintaining the law and administering justice. To reflect this, pharaohs took the title "Beloved of Maat," emphasizing their focus on justice and truth.

17

DEVELOPMENT FOR WHOM?

The eyes can see. The ears can hear. The eyes judge as the ears hear, and the voice tries to speak the language of despair. The eyes see the loud construction cranes deafening their ears in Addis, fighting for life, as the engines of development wake them early in the morning, without anything to look forward to, for the rest of the hot Ethiopian day.

Another day, they say; another night, they add. They see again. They cannot help but see the freezing time around them. As the classic Ethiopian singer said, "Kememot Aldenem," My struggle goes unheeded. All my life I have struggled.

> I struggled to live
> But I also know I am destined to die
> I have carried stones all my life
> Nothing has changed
> I am born to die
> Born to suffer.

So say the eyes of all those poor Ethiopians languishing in Addis. They wake up to the roaring cranes of development, building skyscrapers for the rich, while they soak in the water of poverty and the pool of hopelessness. They say again and again, "I wish I could die, so that I can see the transcendent directly, where I can feel the stillness of time and the sweetness of eternity." But they realize that they are fated to wake up and face the misery of time and space. "Courage, courage," says the voice that must speak. The eyes respond by merely seeing, seeing nothing, except hotels, brothels, mansions for the rich and powerful. They ask again, Where are our leaders? Where is this thing called Maat, about whom our pretentious intellectuals write? For how long are we going to wait, until our leaders acknowledge that we exist, that we are not merely looters but human beings with the right to live? What is even more, they add, Our leaders never tire of telling us that we are developing with the help of the caring state, and we say, "Development for whom?"

FROM

Dekialula, March 7, 2007.

18

MILLENNIUM FOR WHOM?

In "Development for Whom?" (essay no. 43) I bitterly complained that the current philosophy of development that the current regime is following is self-congratulatory, insofar as the development strategies of the present are not changing the lives of the poor of the poorest in contemporary Ethiopia. I am compelled to complain more, now that the Ethiopian media are drunk with the idea of the millennium, as Ethiopia has its own millennium. I now wish to develop this theme further.

Development is profoundly entangled with morality, although the neoliberal model of development seeks to decouple development from morality. Once this decoupling is in place, then regime after regime can ignore the plight of the poor from their radar screens. That is exactly what the so-called development state is doing.

Following this tradition, and falsely claiming a democratic socialist agenda, the prevailing regime in Ethiopia has long ignored the poor by seeking to appease the rich and powerful, up to and including investing billions of dollars on the so-called millennium, to celebrate the whims of the rich, at the expense of the wretched of Ethiopia.

In fact, this phase of Ethiopian history calls not for mindless celebration but for hard-headed moral thinking blended with an appropriate economic form. Modern Ethiopia does not have either. Not only is the regime terrorizing its decent citizens, not only is it starving them, not only is it harassing its brilliant intellectuals, but it is slowly destroying the country by squashing dissent, inhibiting dialogue free of domination, and discouraging reflective Ethiopians from returning home and forming new parties.

The developmental state is developing the rich and powerful in the name of democracy, but it is ignoring its commitment to the poor, who are fighting its unnecessary wars, precisely because it has reductively condensed the idea of development into a sponge that absorbs everything.

Unless development is rethought as a fundamentally moral concept and only peripherally an economic engine, no development state is going to change the lives of the millions of Ethiopians who are burning in the chambers of poverty.

The millennium, if it has any teeth, should focus on starting a genuine strategy of development, since the current regime has none.

From

Dekialula.com, March 7, 2007.

19

THE DEVELOPMENTAL STATE: A CRITICAL ASSESSMENT

In a speech to the African Task Force, at a meeting on August 3 and 4, 2006, Prime Minister Meles Zenawi of Ethiopia gave a tantalizing outline of the contours of a paradigm shift from a neo-liberal view of development to a developmental state. The jargon was arresting and the content was ambiguous. He declared: "The key task in this regard is to transform our political economy from one of pervasive rent-seeking to one that is conducive to value creation…predicated on building the constituency of a developmental state and building the institutions and policy instruments to curtail rent-seeking and promote value creation."

One would have to work hard to decipher the meaning of this jargon to make sense of what the paradigm shift is, since one does not know what rent-seeking and value creations are. The central components of thinking are clarity and respect of language. Most people could surmise what rent-seeking is, but not when it applies to discussing the function of state building, since we do not know who is renting what to whom. This is not merely hair splitting. I am seriously asking for clarity and definitions of a muddled idea, however laudable the vision is.

I like the vision but I am being manipulated to like it, without understanding it. The same muddle applies to a big term, value creation, which is Marxist jargon and a very important one at that; but value creation is not a political term, it is a philosophical/ moral and economic term on which hinges the creation of any commodity that we use, all the way from grains to coffee.

The author must begin with bold and clear definitions of these terms before we are dazzled by the power of rhetoric.

Indeed value creation is the key to a just production, distribution and consumption of any commodity. What is crucial is the analysis of the conditions of the production of commodities, out of which we obtain two kinds of values, use values and exchange values, with different outcomes. Use values do not exploit, whereas exchange values are based on the exploitation of the producers, peasants and urban workers.

Use values create values that are consumed by the primary producers of grains, coffee, shoes, for example. What is produced is immediately consumed by the owner of the commodity.

Exchange values produce values for which the producer is not fully paid. The producer is exploited and the exploitation is naturalized. Neoliberal theory treats exchange value as a natural dimension of the production of exchange value.

The paradigm shift that the author of the developmental state seeks is to lessen the injustices that are inherent in the neoliberal model by reinvigorating, so I hope, the democratic dimension of use values, on which the alternative developmental state can be built.

I have articulated the outlines of future essays that will present a hypothesis of an alternative to the prime minister's vague articulation of an alternative developmental state, which I have discussed in my essays in the past, and are now collected as part of a forthcoming issue in Socialism and Democracy.

From

Dekialula.com, March 14, 2007.

Source

Teodros Kiros and Victor Wallis, eds, *Africa: Philosophy and Social Movements,* Red Sea Press, forthcoming.

20

On Ethiopian National Identity

All Ethiopians can be taught to admire our differences as members of historically generated ethnic groups and as thinking beings, as beings born with the "capacity to think." We can be retaught to trust more and not less, to expunge from the fibers of our being the poison of suspicion and forced unanimity. We Ethiopians should learn how not to hide behind artificial nationalism, a nationalism that does not allow us to freely and courageously criticize our leaders when they make shameful mistakes in our name.

As beings with the capacity to think, we must use this power to peacefully challenge our leaders when they fail to carry out the tasks that we mandated them to perform, and this mission should be articulated without the venom of negative ethnicity (NE).

The Ethiopian people should not be used as pawns the government consults only when they are in trouble. That is treason. It is immoral and politically suicidal. Ethiopians should be permitted to participate in the construction of their nation—free of vengeance and always propelled by political imaginary and moral precision.

Instead, the nationalism and internationalism of Meles is being used destructively, to maintain the position of those in power. Power need not be used as Bonapartism, as Meles shrewdly alleges is the way that the dissidents are using it. One could convincingly argue that Bonapartism is double-pronged, that he himself is as guilty of it as any of his critics. But these attacks and counterattacks are useless in the end as I argued in "When Two Elephants Fight It Is the Grass That Suffers" (essay no. 35). Meles should leave a legacy of a new Ethiopia blessed by the beauty and diversity of a multiethnic state. A multiethnic state, however, must be delinked from negative ethnicity as I argued in "Two Concepts of Ethnicity" (essay no. 39).

An authentic multiethnic state is not nationalistic. Its base ought to be morally educated citizens. Political consciousness is not enough. Political consciousness must wrap itself with moral consciousness. For years, all over the world, particularly in the homelands of vulgar Marxism, citizens have been falsely told that political parties could politically educate them. That is a lie, a shameless lie at that. Nobody can educate another easily. Citizens can educate themselves as moral subjects if they are given the appropriate public sphere, so that they can boldly use their own "public reason." The idea of belonging or not belonging to a nation cannot be taught from the outside. One cannot be told to love ones nation because one is born to it, or more mendaciously because ones kin and blood relations or its race constructed it. We know too well that this is what gullible citizens are told all over the world, to their detriment. Indeed, that is how individuals all over the world are politically miseducated. But it need not be that way, not inexorably. Nothing is permanent. This false sense of belonging, which is what nationalism feeds on, contrary to what some political scientists teach at universities, and which some media writers dignify in their nicely written columns, is neither the complete picture nor carefully thought out. Or, when it is ostensibly worked out, it is done with the end purpose of disenabling the potentially conscious citizens to think for themselves.

Leaders worthy of that name take it upon themselves to demask this process of moral and political miseducation. The leader as a teacher gently not manipulatively heightens the awareness of the citizens through a subtle transformation from nationalism, as an irrational love of the idea of the nation, to national consciousness, as a morally acute sense of the nation. It is the duty of the leader, when called upon, to introduce citizens to the differences between nationalism and consciousness about belonging to a nation.

Rarely, however, are these feelings distinguished for the dizzy citizens smearing the dirt of negative ethnicities, the cousins of narrow nationalism. Where there is no functional government guided by the idea of national consciousness, the true leader provides one. If the existing nation is marred by nationalism and negative ethnicity, the leader replaces that false sense of belonging with a truer one. As Fanon put the matter in *The Wretched of the Earth*, the duty of those at the head of the movement is to have the masses behind them. Allegiance presupposes awareness and understanding of the mission that has to be fulfilled; in short, an intellectual position, however embryonic. We must not voodoo the people, nor dissolve them in emotion and confusion (pp. 199-200). Furthermore, Fanon stresses, "A government which calls itself a national government ought to take responsibility for the totality of the nation" (p. 201).

The present situation in Ethiopia requires the services of a leader who must educate the party he leads and the people who follow him. He must teach again and again. He must not resort to butchery and manipulation when he cannot exact consent and consensus through the art of persuasion. He must free the people from the voodoo of negative ethnicity, intoxication with nationalism, hate and confusion over the direction that the nation should follow. At issue is the perennial question of what a nation is. A nation is composed of individuals with diverse desires and aspirations.

Some of these desires and aspirations are so distinct that they resist the idea of forging a common good to which, when necessary, they have to be sacrificed. Living within a nation of morally and politically conscious individuals requires the creation of a common good. A good is common when the good has something that all the citizens should have, before they can be left free to realize their distinct desires and aspirations. Food, health, shelter and clothing are fundamental goods that all Ethiopian citizens should have, before others who can and should have more, are encouraged to do so.

The common good as the good consisting of health, food, shelter and clothing should not be perceived as coercive, however. The idea of national consciousness should insinuate itself into the moral fibers of individual Ethiopian citizens as a duty. The morally and politically conscious Ethiopians ought not to feel constrained when their government gently guides them to think for others, to embrace the needs of those who live in tin shacks as their very own responsibility to ameliorate. This sense of responsibility has to be created by any means necessary. In modern Ethiopia this good must be distributed by a responsible state to all Ethiopians, and not to particular ethnic groups. National consciousness is embodied in the imperative that the dignity of all Ethiopians should not be the plaything of manipulative politicians who exploit the politics of blood relations and kin.

Nationhood is too precious to simply and plainly be an attribute of nationalism. The future Ethiopian state can come into being only as an activity of national consciousness propelled by an impartial wisdom of a leader mobilizing the resources of a functional state. Ethiopia at the moment is yearning for both. Ethiopia is yearning for a new political party to be led by a genuinely upright individual carrying the torches of Maat, which I will discuss in the next essay.

FROM

Dekialula.com, March 30, 2007.

2 1

The Moral
Imperative of Peace
and the Project of
Development
(Part 1)

Development without war is what the East African Community needs. I would like to defend this thesis. The East
African Community (The Sudan, Ethiopia, Eritrea, Somalia,
Kenya, and Tanzania) needs as a matter of necessity to coordinate
all its resources and develop the entire East African region. That
coordination requires the necessary and sufficient condition of
peace–peace at any cost and by any means necessary.

The moral imperative of peace may initially appear to be an
illusion that cannot produce a reality. Illusions by definition are
just those unrealizable ideals. The moral imperative of peace on
the other hand is not an illusion but rather an idea, or if you prefer,
a guiding ideal, which sets the highest standards of excellence that
humans can realize, if they work at it steadily, tenaciously and
courageously. At a time in which the Western world and parts
of the East African Community are at war over the question of
terrorism, Ethiopia, Eritrea and Somalia have been drawn into
a very costly war that they cannot afford. That the question of
Ethiopian sovereignty is important and that the prevailing regime
in Ethiopia was provoked to enter this war with an extremely poor
neighbor is a political tragedy of our time.

As a political tragedy its impact on the possibilities for the
region are grave, but this gravity could be revisited on different
grounds, the untraveled ground of seeking peace and producing
peace through the force of moral education. Whereas in class-

rooms of universities moral education is conducted by professors of ethics and moral philosophy, it is wise leaders who educate the citizens of nations by the forceless force of vision anchored on ideals. Such is the ideal of the moral imperative of peace, guided by the idea of Maat.

Nothing great, not to say extraordinary, can be achieved without organizing principles. Formulating the thesis syllogistically, we can thus, that economies need organizing principles. The African condition is lacking an organizing principle. Maat can serve as one such principle.

I should now like to elaborate on the syllogism. Maat retains its contemporaneity precisely because humans and their yearning to be moral continues to haunt their consciousness. Humans across the vast stretch of human history have desired to be moral, manifest in all religions, including that of Classical Egypt, which arguably was not organized by a religious doctrine. This claim is not corroborated by research, however; in fact the records by William Budge, hardly an Afrocentrist, but rather an honest Egyptologist, indicate that the gods of Egypt were beholden to AtumRa, the equivalent of the Christian God. Their loving search and their hymns in search of truth inevitably led them to locate Maat, as the home of the transcendent, and that is where they located AtumRa, and they found him in the depths of the human heart/mind, where he dispensed with justice, truth and love.

The late Ato Tsegaye Gebre-Medhin, Ethiopia's greatest poet, sang of this god, from the land of Kush. That is where he located his body. That is where his roots sprouted until they matured in the Ethiopian soil. This search for a self-creating God is one of the constants in human history. This yearning becomes stratophically present during times of material and mental depression.

Classical Egypt also partook in this relentless search for the transcendent, whom it identified as AtumRa. The prophets of Israel and Islam and the preachers of the Christian Bible appeal to a higher force when their situation is flooded by uncontrollable famine, hunger, material and mental depression.

The Psalms are living testaments of human yearning for a higher force to redeem the world, to cleanse the self from hate, jealousy, cruelty and neglect. The Psalms are indeed one long cry of despair, of joy, of love, of hope, of faith and of suffering. To the ancient Egyptians, Maat presented itself as the absolute scale of justice. The best human hearts of the dead were carefully weighed by Maat, and the ones that proved their preciousness were chosen and mummified for eternity. Great were not the pharaohs who were wealthy in material possessions but those who had the weightiest hearts, the ones who exercised their power in accordance with the standard of Maat, the measure of justice.

Contemporary Africa has distanced itself from Classical Egypt. Our leaders, wherever they may be, do not value moral greatness. Governance in contemporary Africa, in spite of the aspiring presence of Maat, an integral part of Africanity, has stripped politics of morality, of truth, of righteousness, of love and of responsibility. Whereas these features are absent among our contemporary leaders, we can revive them, as future features of the next generation. Greatness is being measured by the yardstick of money and the display of wealth. Gone are the days in which greatness, as an ideal, was the fostering of moral and emotional intelligence, which is what Maat, when suitably idealized, symbolized. I advise our civic leaders, priests and other conveyors of core values to introduce their audiences to something like Maat, so that the young can begin to cultivate their moral potentials to their highest possibilities.

The second part of the syllogism states, "The African condition is lacking an organizing principle." Exactly. That organizing principle, I propose, is the concept of Maat. Matt has all the features of a complete moral frame, and I advise African secular educators, civic leaders, religious leaders and others to argue for the imperative that the African condition cannot be revived solely by a spiritless capitalism, but needs a powerful moral force upon which could rest the capitalist engine of profit accumulation. Once the profits are amassed, we need at the helm of the leadership, leaders who would be disciplined by Maat to distribute the wealth equitably. Capitalism arguably may be the accumulator of capital, but it is the most incompetent tool of the moral life. The genius of Maat is that it is a moral force with an implicit economic program that aims at feeding, clothing and sheltering the children of humanity, without pitying humans against others. The economic form is implicit in the moral form, and that moral form has yet to be articulated.

I propose to our leaders that they consider Maat as the appropriate moral form that could produce the practical idea of the moral imperative of peace for the East African Community of the immediate future.

From
Dekialula.com, January 5, 2007.
Source
William Budge.

22

THE MORAL IMPERATIVE OF PEACE AND THE PROJECT OF DEVELOPMENT (PART 2)

It is precisely indispensable civic attributes that the target population—Eritrean, Ethiopian, Somali, Sudanese youth (ages 6-20) in Boston, Chelsea and Cambridge, Massachusetts are significantly lacking. All are very low or low-income and roughly 80% live in low-income neighborhoods in Chelsea, Roxbury, Dorchester, North Cambridge and Quincy. While our constituents are from diverse nations with different cultural and linguistic backgrounds, many of them share the same legacy of violence, death, poverty and displacement. Fleeing civil wars, economic dislocation, environmental degradation and/or ethnic persecutions at home, the majority of our African refugees/immigrants arrive in the United States sharing a similar emotional and psychological profile. Regardless of national origin, our youth face similar educational inequities.

Civil war and severe periodic economic downswings, if not hardships, often disrupt formal schooling in African countries. Oftentimes, our African refugees/immigrants are women with children, usually from middle to high school age. Many have received little, if any, education in their homelands and illiteracy rates are high. The majority of these women have illnesses and physical and/or psychological disabilities related to poor nutrition and health care, female genital mutilation, violence, economic hardship and limited technology skills.

Many of our youth have had minimal education while others have never been to school until their arrival in the Boston public school system. Because school placement is based on age, African youth struggle to keep up with limited educational experience and borderline English competency in high school. The majority of our students reside in the Boston Empowerment Zone, the various secondary schools of which are among the poorest performing in recent citywide tests, as well as on the state-mandated Massachusetts Comprehensive Assessment System (MCAS) exams.

Declining MCAS scores and the attendant problem of graduating high school are additional areas of need ACEDONE (African Community Economic Development of New England) hopes to address in plans currently being prepared for year four of operation. Besides a lack of parent/guardian involvement in their children's education, a seemingly ubiquitous "generation gap" is manifest. It is apparent in the digital divide between students' limited knowledge and implementation of multimedia technology and their parent/guardian's lack of use or understanding of the same. Between students and adults there are often tenuous lines of communication. Past experiences and cultural norms in the target population frequently combine to produce a marked resistance to knowledge of, or interest in, civic engagement.

Our collaborative works form the premise that participation in the political process is a right and responsibility, and that we can be particularly effective in assisting new arrivals to negotiate this cultural impasse. Additional areas of concern among our adolescents include unfamiliarity with employment procedures and application processes. Often there is a palpable need for more attention to the development of conflict resolution and people skills in an urban, multicultural environment. Outdoor activities are bound to help them to interact with one another as they play sports outside of the confines of the classroom and learn how to become leaders and organizers of their communities.

FROM

Dekialula.com, March 24, 2007.

23

LITERATURE AND DIGNITY

Medicine is to the body, as good literature is to the soul. During turbulent times, such as ours, once in a while a book appears on the horizon to enlighten us, expand our horizons, stretch our imaginations and sometimes gently challenge us to readjust our cultural lenses by forcing us to think anew, and to travel on uncharted waters. The book under review in this essay does all of the above with remarkable adroitness and deftness of the writing hand.

Somalia, once an ancient city-state of the East African world, which in recent times has been hit hard by the tragedies of war, squalor and early death of its relentless people, has just been rewarded with a powerful literary presence, of a book that seeks to expose the achievements of its heroic people to the cynical world.

The reward is by a young emerging author, Mr. Anwar Maxamed Diiriye, *Literature of Somali Onomastics and Proverbs*. The book is organized around explorations of the meaning of indigenous names, and an exhibition of Somali and English proverbs. Both topics are amply rewarding. They are first-rate treatments of important themes in the understanding of the cultural history of a unique nation that shares the glorious past history of the Arab world and the living fountains of the African world.

An understanding of contemporary Somalia challenges us to come to terms with a historic nation seeking to determine its rich history by paying homage to Islam, Arabism and Africanity, since Somalia partakes the horizons of a triple heritage.

Chapter one introduces us to the Somali nomenclature system, in which any Somali name is followed by the father's name, and the grandfather's. Women retain their names even after marriage. The original names are either Cushitic (African) or Arabic. All Somali names are organized around qualities (white), and names that ward off the evil eye. Women's names in contrast are categorized by physical or moral attributes. All the names however have meaning. Parents and others are provided with meaning and destiny-bearing qualities from which they could choose, when they want to name their precious offspring. The nomenclature is one huge depository of identities.

Chapter two delves deeply into Arabic or Islamic names. The attributes of Allah are the ideals that name-givers yearn for as they want to grace their children with a holy name, hoping that names will map out the destinies of their children. . Such names are collected in the Quran (Hadith). Great are the names that are available in the Hadith so that proud parents can locate them and choose them as the blessed names of their children. For example, Abdul means servant of the most gracious. Such is the living power of the second chapter that introduces the reader to a wealth of names, which are simultaneously identity providers, and meaningful conveyors of tradition, customs and history of the Somali nation.

Chapters three and four are intricate and brilliant mediators of meaning, instruction and philosophical orality, which are particularly useful to all those cynical outsiders who think that there is no African philosophy. This important book proves that that there is indeed a philosophical sagacity of a Cushitic and Arabic origin in Somalia's cultural soil. Witness its presence by buying this book and reading it for yourselves.

Consider the following proverbs as mediators of philosphical insight, which are analytic and ethical at the same time:

> Wisdom is content out of the knowledge "Science."
> A nation with no archives is like eyes without sight "Vision."
> God's grace does not come in a day's duration.
> Prevention is better than cure.

These proverbs and hundreds like them are a wealth of philosophical instruction that we must read. This is a great book written by a very bright young man, and to whom I say thanks for giving me the honor to review.

FROM

Dekialula.com, April 4, 2007.

SOURCE

Anwar Maxamed Diiriye, *Literature of Somali Onomastics and Proverbs*, Gobaad Communications & Press, Minneapolis, MN, 2006.

24

The Struggle On Kennedy Road in South Africa: A Model for Poor People in the Rest of Africa

In an article in *Socialism and Democracy*, Nigel Gibson wrote: "On March 19th 2005, in a scene reminiscent of the anti-apartheid struggle, 750 black shack dwellers barricaded a major ring road in Durban, fighting the police for four hours. By this time the shack dwellers had been waiting patiently for Nelson Mandela's historic 1994 election promise of housing to be realized. These promised houses were to be built on a nearby piece of land."

I say hail to poor people, all those poor shack dwellers in Ethiopia, which is my focus here. I say again rise against all those who are keeping you down, all the rich and powerful who are sipping the delicious coffee that you produce with your unpaid labor; all those forces of power that refuse to free your AIDS-infected bodies from pain and sorrow.

Your South African sisters and brothers are setting a revolutionary example for you. The moral and political reorganization of your shattered selves demands that you march to the public sphere and act, act now and dream later.

You must not live without basic necessities; food, shelter, clothing, coal. You must not live with big rats ready to devour your vulnerable bodies. Do not merely wait for politicians to promise the delivery of goods, without which you cannot live. Say no to empty promises. Organize, act, plan and march on the unpaved streets of shantytowns. Revolt against betrayal. Make revolution-ary time against idle time. Make time serve your condition. Use space and time to fight for your rights. The rich say you are poor, but you are not poor. You are rich in mind, in spirit, in honesty and in courage. Use these virtues and change your situation.

The South African struggle now is a living example of what other Africans can and must do. The poor of the African condition are the same.

FROM

Dekialula.com, December 26, 2006.

SOURCE

Nigel Gibson, "Zabalaza, Unfinished Struggles Against Apartheid: The Shackdwellers' Movement in Durban" in a special issue of, *Socialism and Democracy, Africa: Philosophy, Social Movements and Politics,* edited by Teodros Kiros and George Katsiaficas, July 16, 2007.

25

WAR AND DEVELOPMENT

Whereas rich nations can afford to go to war, in spite of the immorality of the action, poor nations suffer twice and more severely than rich nations because

1. They can not materially afford to finance any war.
2. If they could be given money by richer nations to go to war, it is…
3. Immoral and foolish to misuse the aid money to sponsor wars, when the money...
4. Could be used to finance very much needed development projects in the third world.

Development understood in several complex ways almost always cannot coexist with the desire to go to war. Of course, one could cynically argue that when a nation's sovereignty is unjustly violated and that nation's population demands that sovereignty comes before peace, then leaders are forced to go to war to satisfy the population's just demands. Under such severe contingencies, going to war becomes a political necessity, but even under this severe condition, one could easily imagine alternatives of removing the political need of going to war by other means. It is the duty of leaders to reason out both the conditions under which a nation should go to war and the conditions under which the demands of development with peace should be attended. When there is an angry population the leader can be forced to go to war to restore peace and bring calm to the nation; when the population is not as angry but simply anxious and inflamed by the pangs of hunger and the brutality of poverty, the leader must fetch peace with prosperity under any condition. I call this the imperative of moral education for the sake of development.

FROM

Dekialula.com, November 18, 2007.

26

Artist/
Dr. Telahun
Gessese:
The Thunderous
Voice of the King
of Ethiopian Music

Joy. Laughter. Dance and more dance. Pride and tradition, modernity and classicism. These are the languages of the Ethiopian youth and some of their parents on this cold winter night as they jubilantly flood the dance floor.

The dance floor at a huge hall is readied to accommodate over a thousand people bursting with the exuberance of youth, the fire of joy, the swings and twists of modern Ethiopian dance responding to the groveling multicultural band of a Caucasian trumpeter, an oriental clarinet and an Ethiopian female singer dominated this winter night in the city of Watertown, Massachusetts, on December 9, 2006.

The king of Ethiopian music is hidden somewhere in the background. The crowd, which knows his lurking presence, is anxious with apprehension, for it knows that the handsome man from the land of AtumRa, the Egyptian transcendent, about whom the late king of Ethiopian poetry, Mr. Ato Tsegaye Gebre-Medhin wrote, is lurking in the background–living music, quietly singing its verses, endlessly perfecting the performance for the historic night and drinking from the endless well of wisdom and love.

The crowd also wants to quench its thirst by drinking from the king's music, the king's passion. He is there in the back, but nowhere to be seen.

The music roars on, and youth dance with hips swinging, shoulders vibrating and legs moving gracefully and carrying the anxious bodies of hundreds of Ethiopians patiently waiting for the appearance of the king himself.

The doctor of music holds on and keeps the crowd waiting. Dance. More dance. Shouts and more shouts. The music roars on and the saxophone is going out of control.

Finally, a man, larger than life, firmly planted in a wheelchair, makes his way to the center of the stage, and the seated audience of Ethiopian celebrities leave their seats, rise and walk to the ends of the stage and salute and pay their tribute to Dr. Telahun Gessese, the Ethiopian genius, the man who has no match, and whose feet will never be filled by another singer's shoes.

He is Ethiopian music at the height of its perfection, and the depth of its living wisdom. With him music is philosophy and philosophy itself attains the musicality that the ancients have yearned for. For in his slender hands music becomes a therapy for those whose hearts have been broken by love, for all those who know the dangers of love and still dare to taste its bitter/sweet pills. To them he has come to sing this night in a wheel chair reserved for all those geniuses that God has chosen for one of his hidden missions toward the last part of their living lives.

The king of music has been chosen for a mission and he carries it out with a biting courage and embodied it with an extraordinary intelligence of the human heart.

Of medium height, with a chiseled nose, a long face and an arresting complexion, the doctor /artist sits on and sings to eternity. Love, death, sorrow, purpose, silence, solitude and the joy that kills are the themes of his heartbreaking songs. He grabs the microphone so close to his soul and projects that voice, which refuses to die in the air, until the listener is driven to tears and the heart is threatened with the possibility of death. His music is fated to bring the audience to the brink of joy, the joy that could kill, and the fulfillment that makes you move toward God. His music is spiritual and carnal, therapeutic and transcendental, which takes you behind the veil of appearance to the depth of the hidden reality.

Yes, he sings tirelessly as he has for the last decades as the king of Ethiopian music.

The night is over and the reluctant crowd parts with respect and gratefulness to the transcendent for implanting this man in the Ethiopian soil, and now as he moves toward death, he is crowned with the mission to serve, to do the Lord's work, and so I am lucky to breakfast with him at the Red Sea, Boston's premier Ethiopian restaurant, shortly before he left.

When we meet there on a sunny Sunday, he muses for over an hour and a half about music and its vocation. His mission now is to open a clinic for the victims of diabetes, the very disease that confined him to a wheelchair, from where, a night before, he sang with arresting brilliance, candor and purposefulness of a young man, born to sing with the vigor of agelessness.

Participating in a long debate about the role of the artist in the age of "mechanical reproduction," he argues compellingly that for him, "the artist is a harbinger of change, a moral mediator of human values, and that his long dream has been to fight for the bricklayers, the gold and silversmiths and the lowly paid soldiers and maids who break their backs to make a living and are then stereotyped by the rich and powerful as unfit and unqualified to marry whomever they love by being cast away as the untouchable."

He continues, "I have attempted to play a part in restoring their dignities, and now their children are in visible political spaces running administrative centers of power, all the way from the palace to the modern bureaucracies." His classic song "Kememot Aldenem" does indeed herald their names and sing their praises, and they in turn give him the tragic thematics of his songs, delivered with inimitable voice, clear and deep– for the last fifty-three years. For he began singing at the tender of age eleven, and has not stopped since. He remembers those early years fondly.

He praises all those artists of the past, from Germany to the USA, who used art to be the mediator of meaning without losing its autonomy and serving the whims of powerholders; he praises even more all those Ethiopian artists of the past who fought for the poor by making them present in our consciences and our lives. For him, "Art is both free and restrained, it is free to create out of the imagination by constructing its own laws of beauty and standards of excellence, and restrained by the commitment to the public, its joys and pains and its dreams and frustrations."

He uses art as autonomous and engaged, private and public. What pleases him most is the presence of the young who come to see him, to touch him and on whom he attempts to pass on his unfulfilled mission of fighting for the afflicted, the poor, the over-burdened, the alienated and all those who are languishing inside the gates of poverty.

At one weak moment he cries and says, "In spite of the limited numbers of those who came, I am lucky that I have seventy-five million Ethiopians backing me in my endeavor to do the Lord's work, which is service to Ethiopian humanity, service to art and the artist as a social agent, as a purposeful mediator of truth and justice in the right way and at the right time. Ethiopians are my social capital, the source and foundations of my music. How much I long to open a school on the human voice, so that the tradition of classical Ethiopian music could be passed on across generations."

The king is moved by the hundreds of youth who stretch their longing hands to touch the genius' soul by feeling his tender and loving hands. They stood by him adoringly, they took pictures of him for remembrance of things past. Some cried. Some froze with hypnotized stares, and many danced almost to death. He remem-bers them all with eyes filled with unshed tears, he remembers them because they vindicate him, because they know first hand the power of Eros, the urge to create by always being behind the limits of experience, where art meets danger, and where life risks death, for the sake of creating and following the silent laws of beauty, of tragedy and death itself.

Toward the end, Mr. Bekele and Ms. Misrak, the generous owners of the Red Sea Restaurant, and Mr. Tadesse, the distin-guished owner of Quality@Your Service, a very close friend of the artist/doctor, and I push the wheelchair on which sat the king of Ethiopian music up from the basement floor, and thus leaves the voice of love, of hope and of faith.

FROM

Dekialula.com, December 26, 2007.

27

MEDITATIVE THINKING AND MORAL ECONOMY

Meditative thinking is a crucial dimension of moral economy; indeed, when suitably theorized, it is the foundation of moral life. Meditative thinking organizes the self's interior constitution by providing the desiring self the necessary pillars of moral organization. When the self is harassed by the pangs of desire, and by the meandering flows of endless yearning for things, the meditative moral cast regulates the uncontrollable urge to own things, to possess commodities, to exploit people. It is precisely meditation, which is the media of communication of the self with the self, which puts the self at ease and deals with its own internal conflicts before the self gets out of its cocoon to live with others.

Prior to living with others, the self must first learn the art of living with its very self in the loneliness of everyday life. Meditation shows us the way of freeing ourselves from the hold of the ego, the self-obsessed ego. The citizens of the new moral economy must learn how to care for the self by making meditation the only way of communicating with the transcendent in the solitude of silence. Silence is the way of meditation. The self must learn how to empty itself from the burdens of business and sit and think- to free itself from the gripping power of busybodies.

When we are pervaded by silence, we are then forced to enter the deep recesses of our souls and think freely. Freedom in a deep sense begins at that stage in which the self frees itself from self obsession and recognizes that there are other selves who need our consistent attention, our patient care and our loving tolerance of their ways and their needs.

The self should be free from the pressures of the ego, so that it can open itself to the mysteries and challenges of the world.

Self-hurt is replaced by self-help. The bruises of jealousy and envy are displaced by the loving presence of understanding and joy. The future members of the new moral economy ought to incorporate meditative thinking as they live within the confines of the moral community– attending to the African condition.

FROM

Dekialula.com, October 5, 2007.

28

SILENCE AND MORAL ECONOMY

Silence is a space, an empty space; silence is a space waiting for an extraordinary nothingness, the creator of all things, the transcendental itself. Silence is the space of the no-thing. The modern life of busy things has no space for silence; our everyday lives are filled with things.

The streets are crowded; the trams are congested; the buses teem with people; the restaurants are busy. Silence has no place in modern life, with the harassed single mother of three or more children making ends meet; the divorced husband working away at three jobs for more child support to pay; the millionaire breaking his back to become a billionaire; the tenured professor moving on up to the presidency of a major university; the third world professor driving a cab at night to feed a family. With these human beings and countless others struggling to stay alive, silence is not there, solitude is absent.

The new moral economy must free these busybodies from the burdens of excessive work, from self-imposed tutelage to the power of material things. The modern citizen of a moral economy must be given ample time to witness bees making honey, roses blooming into life, snow falling in the middle of the night, trees carrying chirping birds, the ocean waves forming caravans of lines of beauty.

We must train ourselves to walk in the silver meadows of thought, to meet the transcendent in the silence of solitude, the grace of hope, the envelope of love, the lake of patience, the pools of prayers and the wraps of compassion and care.

Through paid holidays and shortened workdays, the citizens of the new moral economy must learn the ways of thought, the stylistics of engaged citizenship. The engaged citizens of the future moral economy think and act morally. They are existentially serious, they think for others. The solitude of silence releases them to welcome the presence of the transcendent. They attend to the harmonious relationship of their bodies and minds. Patience and laughter are on their fingertips. They experience life lightly.

The silence of thought guides their moral actions. They work less and think more. Lakes, rivers, brooks, walks and the company of friends are their abodes. The new moral economy bolsters them by giving them ample time to develop their virtues and cleanse their vices. They release themselves from the sway of commodities toward the silent presence of the transcendent, who gives them the gentle laws of moral life, the laws that put them on the correct moral path, paving the way for the emergence of existential seriousness, the subject of the next essay.

From

Dekialula.com, November 14, 2007.

29

EXISTENTIAL
SERIOUSNESS

In "A Democratic Citizen" (essay no. 94) I write, "Why do we have looters?" This is precisely an existential and developmental question that the policy makers need to address, now that they have secured power; and similarly the opposition leaders need to start immediately to develop a coherent program of addressing all those complicated causes of looting, idling, prostitution and fatal diseases. I challenge both the existing regime and the aspiring political parties of the future to develop genuine developmental programs guided by existential seriousness and moral intelligence.

I would like to develop this argument further. Existential seriousness is the view that human lives are sacrosanct and that no regime has the right to violate the dignity of the human being who is fated to die, and the inevitability of death itself imposes an imperative on regimes to feed, clothe and shelter all those citizens who find themselves inside states who starve, kill and impoverish them. Existential seriousness extends moral and material attention to their daily lives consistently and compassionately. Compassion, care and principles are the pillars of existence. When one takes one's existence seriously, the preciousness of being alive is not taken for granted. All human and nonhuman lives are respected and loved. Killing any being is not taken lightly. Existence is experienced as a moral firmament, framed inside the fortress of an ethics and aesthetics of living. All humans and nonhumans are honored and their dignities are revered with a magnificent language of deep respect. We hail only those regimes that take the preciousness of existence seriously, and do not negotiate human lives for state security.

Genuinely democratic states ought to develop developmental programs propelled by moral intelligence and anchored on existential seriousness as I have defined it. Human lives are not to be negotiated for a state's security measures, as was recently done by the prevailing regime in Ethiopia. Looters, prostitutes, hooligans, whatever name the regime gives them, are the subjects of existential seriousness. These Ethiopians are the children of the transcendent, the force who created them out of nothing, the reflective presence, who creates others, without creating itself. When human existence is measured by the precious yardstick of existential seriousness, all human lives are so spiritually precious that no materialistic developmental project can justify their annihilation. The recent events in Ethiopia have violated the moral contours of existential seriousness, and the governing regime better think twice before committing another crime, because those whose lives have been taken away, and the beloved ones who are mired in grief, are shouting the language of tragedy, the spiritual child of existential seriousness. Future shouts must be combated against by the masses themselves, as critical revolutionary activity, on behalf of the sanctity of life, the special dignity of all those who exist, only because they are already fated to die. That fate is enough to justify their inherent right to live the good life, while alive, a possibility of existence mapped out for them by the just transcendent. That possibility of life cannot be taken away by any regime, as was done by the governing party.

I hope that this will be the last time human lives are obliterated for nothing. No security measure, no political exigency, no developmental imperative, no ethnically motivated lies are going to be employed to erase human existence, given the preciousness of existence itself. No regime has the right to annihilate the children of the transcendent under the rubric of a manufactured lie that the regime was only killing hooligans and protecting the wealth of the rich and the materially advantaged. Looters also have the right to live. They are the moral subjects of existential seriousness. Only the reflective presence of the transcendent above has the ultimate right to pass final judgment on the quality and quantity of their existence. Regimes, revolutionary or not, do not have such a right. If they have any right at all it is to feed, shelter, clothe and maintain the health of all citizen subjects.

From

Dekialula.com, August 18, 2005.

30

Existential Seriousness and Political Culture

I cry for my country as the specters of death, blood bath, insurrection and heroic moments of political struggle are haunting this mountainous presence in East Africa, the birthplace of humanity.

Once again the reasonable imperatives of existential seriousness have been flagrantly violated and the nation's emerging new political culture is at peril. I have in many previous essays argued that the sovereignty of the individual Ethiopian, rich and poor, learned and illiterate, young and old, men and women is so precious that no nation has the right to violate it. Every single Ethiopian has an inherent right to determine their individual existence, and the sovereignty of the places of their origin, in whatever form the political practice is expressed. The form and content of political action cannot be determined by the state. Political practices must be chosen by the political actors at a given time, a given place, in the right form and for the right reason. Occasionally, political forms, particularly in the hands of the young and inexperienced, do take violent forms, but that is no reason for a state to kill the protestors and imprison their organizers.

The motto of existential seriousness is the carefully thought-out belief that the sovereign individual is the child of the transcendent and the state has no right to kill this individual, however compelling the political necessities might be. To kill these beacons of change, harbingers of dreams, is to kill both the dreams and the sovereign hearts in which these dreams originate.

The highly important virtues of a contemporary Ethiopian citizen are courage and justice. These virtues need the nurturing help of a compassionate and confident regime, and not whips, guns and knives. Considering the developmental conditions in the country, particularly poverty, disease and political alienation, the revolutionary values that revolutionary democracy preached, and which the citizens (both the new party's leaders and their followers) took seriously, are being used effectively against the existing regime to change its way, if not to get out of the way.

These courageous moments of political action need to be hailed as new political forms of an emerging political culture, the chief features of which are protest on the streets, conscientious objections and prayer at home and at churches. These nuanced forms of resistance are markers of an emerging political culture of the previously excluded Ethiopian citizens.

All these practices are stylistics of heroism, expressions of ways of life and a relentless demand for change, up to and including contesting "rigged outcomes" of political elections. The regime in power should be proud to have nurtured courageous political actors, ready to die for a way of life, an ethics and aesthetics of existence. These are the virtues of vigilant citizens of the modern Ethiopian polis. Protests are propelled by a profound understanding of political duty and one learns how to be dutiful by doing dutiful things. Along the way many mistakes are made, and those who have never protested before make grave mistakes. But they can learn only by making mistakes, and their leaders do take chances as they work these young voices of freedom, of hope, of change and of yearning for the end to poverty, neglect, diseases and political alienation. They want to form new political parties. That is their inherent right, a right conferred to them by their existential seriousness. It is that right that is being taken away, when their leaders are being imprisoned, and their political imaginations aborted before they mature in the hands of time, and in the extremely limited political space that the regime is allowing them.

Should their leaders be imprisoned and their followers killed and provoked to kill others only because they are engaging in a new political culture of imagination, courage and a desperate search for a new regime, and a new political party?

From

Dekialula.com, November 14, 2005.

3 1

EXISTENTIAL SERIOUSNESS AND HUMAN RIGHTS IN CONTEMPORARY ETHIOPIA

On August 17, 2008, I wrote in *Dekialula*.com:

> Existential seriousness is the view that human lives are sacrosanct and that no regime has the right to violate the dignity of the human being who is fated to die, and the inevitability of death itself imposes an imperative on regimes to feed, clothe and shelter all those citizens who find themselves inside states that starve, kill and impoverish them. Existential seriousness extends moral and material attention to their daily lives consistently and compassionately. Compassion, care and principles are the pillars of existence. When one takes one's existence seriously, the preciousness of being alive is not taken for granted. All human and nonhuman lives are respected and loved. Killing any being is not taken lightly. Existence is experienced as a moral firmament, framed inside the fortress of an ethics and aesthetics of living. All humans and nonhumans are honored and their dignities are revered with a magnificent language of deep respect.

> We hail only those regimes that take the preciousness of existence seriously, and do not negotiate human lives for state security. Genuinely democratic states ought to have developmental programs propelled by moral intelligence and anchored on existential seriousness as I defined it above. Human lives are not to be

negotiated for a state's security measures, as is being done by the prevailing regime in Ethiopia. Looters, prostitutes, hooligans, whatever name the regime gives them, are the subjects of existential seriousness. These Ethiopians are the children of the transcendent, the force who created them out of nothing, the reflective presence, who creates others, without creating itself. When human existence is measured by the precious yardstick of existential seriousness, all human lives are so spiritually precious that no materialistic developmental project can justify their annihilation.

The recent events in Ethiopia have violated the moral contours of existential seriousness, and the governing regime better think twice before committing another crime, because those whose lives have been taken away, and the beloved ones who are mired in grief, are shouting the language of tragedy, the spiritual child of existential seriousness. Future shouts must be combated against by the masses themselves, as a critical revolutionary activity, on behalf of the sanctity of life, the special dignity of all those who exist, only because they are already fated to die. That fate is enough to justify their inherent right to live the good life, while alive, a possibility of existence mapped out for them by the just transcendent. That possibility of life cannot be taken away by any regime, as was done by the governing party.

These words have now gained a poignant contemporaneity in light of the international attention that the politics of the election is exacting. In 2005, 193 protestors, many of whom were students, died while exercising their constitutionally guaranteed right to protest, and the imprisonment of their leaders violated the higher existential right of the children of the transcendent. My argument is that had the regime restrained itself even more, the unnecessary deaths and the controversial imprisonment of leaders could have saved the regime from the impending international trial that is being set against those who masterminded the postelection turmoil in this poverty and AIDS-ravished historic East African nation.

The recent world attention of the deaths of the 193 Ethiopians has now put the regime at loggerheads against the international community. Both the violation of human rights and the deeper violation of existential right to a future life have been barbarically violated. This violation should warn those who are planning to replace the existing regime that they too may one day be tempted to do the same, when those who are in power now are removed and new players take their place. Unless we train those who are calling for change to learn how to negotiate power sharing by democratic discourse free of domination, there is absolutely no guarantee that they too would use force, a prepolitical instrument of regime barbarism, to originate, develop and defend ideas against their opponents.

Recklessness as practiced by the regime in power, and the opposition, which continues to threaten its use, succumb to a pre-civilzational state of war, which is neither wanted nor productive, as we witness in contemporary Ethiopian politics. Force is a prepolitical instrument that violates the existential right of citizens, whereas disciplined dialogue nurtures citizens out of otherwise intimidated and docile subjects. Docile subjects are prone to early death, because they are afraid to stand up and fight for their rights, whereas confident citizens articulate their rights and die for them, as existentially serious. Confident citizens radiate with the presence of the transcendent, who shows them the way, by putting them on the right moral/political path, lovingly and patiently. It is this vision of existential seriousness that the future contenders of power must internalize so as not to trample on the human rights of existentially serious citizens. The future life of existentially serious Ethiopians should not be jeopardized either by the regime in power or by the opposition that is seeking to come to power. The human rights of Ethiopians are beyond the divisive and ethnic language of contemporary Ethiopian politics. The ones who protest are the ones who do so suffused with the presence of the transcendent, showing them the way, guiding them, correcting them. Existentially serious leaders of the masses should themselves radiate with the rapturous sense of political responsibility blended with the political imagination of autonomous reason.

The ongoing behavior of the Ethiopian opposition is marred by the temptations of prepoliticality or responding to violence and negative ethnicity with counterviolence and counterethnicity, which must be stopped, otherwise contemporary Ethiopian politics will enter into a vicious cycle, from which we Ethiopians will never extricate ourselves. Now that the International Court and other organizations, have woken up from their sleep, and are paying tribute to the violation of the human rights of black bodies, we Ethiopians also should wake up to how badly we are treating each other, and change our ways now.

Now is the time. The time for soul searching is now, and not later.

FROM
Dekialula.com, July 19, 2006.

32

ECONOMIC FORM: THE PLACE OF THE HEART IN MORAL ECONOMY

The Egyptians have held the human heart at a level beyond any other organ, and this decision is not an accident. They revered the heart and mummified it, whereas the brain was sucked out and thrown away at death. Whereas modern medicine continues to treat the brain as the cognitive organ that originates and processes thoughts, the ancient Egyptians treated the human heart as the seat of thinking. To the Egyptians the human heart had both a physical and transcendental function, its physical function is pumping blood and its transcendental function is moral thought; whereas to modern medicine the human heart is exclusively a physical organ, without any transcendental task, it simply pumps blood through the intricate interiors of the heart. Maat was guided by the human heart as the seat of thinking. The seated Egyptian philosopher, who internalized Maat, originated generosity, justice, wisdom, curiosity and tolerance from the heart. The heart is the home of thought impulses, or what we loosely call feelings.

To the Egyptians, the heart is primarily the seat of thinking. They accorded weight to its transcendental function. The Egyptians reasoned that thoughts originated in the heart, and the brain processes those thoughts, and the thoughts are emitted as language. Some thoughts are expressed as speech and others are buried in the depth of the unconscious, beyond language, the realm of the expressible. It is the Egyptian insight about the heart as the seat of thinking, particularly moral thinking, that recommends the heart to have a central place in moral economy.

The citizens of the new moral economy must be encouraged to practice what they intuitively know, that moral thinking is both thinking outside of the self and the attempt at reaching the unknown and perhaps unknowable other. This difficult task of embracing another person's concerns as your very own is precisely the territory that the human heart undertakes. The brain indeed processes those thoughts, moral and otherwise, that originate in that regime of transcendental thought, but the depth of the need to embrace the other, to think for the other and with the other, are practices in moral thinking that we feel deeply in our hearts; the will propels us toward action, and the brain organizes the sequences of what must be done.

The new moral economy must make the heart the leader of action, and citizens must be encouraged to take the language of the heart, namely feeling, much more seriously. Where these intuitively felt and lived thoughts are temporarily absent from our busy lives, they must be made present by being remembered and recollected as the citizen's habits. Where they are absent they must be made present through systematic education at schools, madrassas, churches and other institutions of modern society.

The new moral economy desperately needs thoughtful human beings. Here is one such place where the moral training of such citizens could begin as a project for the future of a functional moral economy. A functional moral economy does not only need leaders who follow the ways of Maat, but much more important are citizens who practice what they feel in their hearts, or who at the minimum know intuitively that is what they must do, if they are to preserve the human species. Maat shows us the way and the human heart demonstrates the value of the practice.

From

Dekialula.com, October 5, 2006.

110

33

MORAL ECONOMY

Sir. Francis Bacon, the renowned English poet, writes about uprightness:

> A man of life upright
> Whose guiltless heart is free,
> From all dishonest deeds,
> Or thoughts of vanity.

The Hindi word *Arjava* means uprightness, straightforwardness, simplicity, frank-speaking, honesty, nonhypocrisy, large-heartedness and freedom from deceit. I have argued previously that justice is a foundational pillar of Maat, and that acting justly does not demand that the person who wants to act justly must first know what justice is. Following Aristotle's *Nichomachean Ethics* (Book Five), I argued instead that acting justly is a habit born out of practice–that is, a repeated practice. Given the practice, acting justly comes quite naturally.

I should now complicate this discussion by introducing the role of uprightness and honesty to the picture. Previously, I have used the case of cutting a pie to exact pieces to make the point that it is the moral fame of the person who has been chosen to cut the pie, who determines the outcome of the exercise, that unless the cutter herself is just, the outcome of the task will not be just. To that view I now add the further requirement that that person must not only be just, in that she cuts the pie into several equal parts, but she is also additionally upright or honest. The component of justice is further strengthened by the feature of uprightness.

Working that example further, a new and more complicated picture emerges. To begin with, how do I understand uprightness before I proceed to use it freely? The English poet whom I copied is right when he emphasized that uprightness feeds on the freedom of the heart and the conquest of vanity. Both conditions must be present for uprightness to illuminate the paths of justice. Thus the just person not only respects the principle of equality but also works on her soul to cleanse herself of the vileness of the unfree heart and the poison of vanity. So are the Hindi thinkers right, when they also stress that straightforwardness, simplicity, frank-speaking, honesty, nonhypocrisy and large heartedness are mastered by practice? This is very much as Aristotle taught us, when he instructed that all the virtues are known by doing them as opposed to simply knowing them, that true knowing is doing and not merely knowing what one should do. The first is easy, and the second so hard that we shun away from it, discouraged by the weight of the task.

So the just person must also cultivate uprightness as a stylistic and ethic of existence. The care of the moral self requires uprightness as a fundamental virtue, a virtue that significantly supplements justice. The just cutter of the pie does her task well because her disposition is already honesty and humility.

FROM

Dekialula.com, October 5, 2006.

34

MORAL ECONOMY: AN ALTERNATIVE TO CAPITALISM AND SOCIALISM

Maat was to ancient Egypt as wisdom was to ancient Greece. Wisdom was to Plato's Aristocratic regime as Maat was to Egypt's social and political life. The concept of Maat insinuated itself with every aspect of Classical Egypt. Pharaohs and the majestic slaves who erected the pyramids swore by Maat. Rich and poor, men and women, slaves and free citizens worshipped the magic of Maat. Maat was the moral organizer of everyday life in classical Egypt. Every facet of Egyptian life was organized by the expansive principle of Maat. Every facet of Egyptian life was framed by Maat. Why did Maat have such a presence in Egyptian life? What was its magical spell? I should now like to address these questions. The human self requires an organizing moral principle. Moral life cannot function without a moral frame, a frame that furnishes the self with boundaries and limiting conditions of social action. It is precisely this lacuna that was lacking in Egyptian morality until the self-creating Egyptian gods originated the expansive concept of Maat. Maat was symbolized by the feminine principle of "truth, balance, order and justice." Maat was harmony, righteousness, patience and vision, born out of the feminine principle of patient labor. For the ancient Egyptians, the order of the universe was also the ideal order for the human world.

For the Greeks, the universe was ordered by Logos, by the rational word. It is this order that Plato used in his *Republic*, when he constructed an ideal city out of Logos. This principle was later translated into "In the beginning was Logos," and was with God and the Logos was God (John1:1). Jesus himself was Logos. In marked contrast, for the ancient Egyptians, the organizing principle of Logos was replaced by the organizing principle of Maat. The Egyptian city was ruled by kings who personified Maat. The human heart, which was worshipped by the Egyptians, and which was the seat of thinking, was also the seat of Maat. The pharaohs were expected to rule with Maat, and not without it. The pharaohs' greatness was measured by the quality and quantity of Maat that he or she internalized. After death, their hearts would be weighed by the scale of Maat, the scale of justice.

When famines occurred and deep inequalities became a way of life, it was the duty of the rulers to uphold Maat and measure the depth and extent of the suffering. Not that this ideal was perfectly upheld, particularly when nature overwhelmed the rulers' ideals, but there was at least an absolute and objective standard by which social/political life was judged and measured.

Maat as a moral form requires an appropriate economic form, which has yet to be theorized. I should now like to defend the following hypothesis: No matter how elastic and flexible the dominant capitalist economic form, and however generously it is stretched, the capitalist economic form is plainly speaking morally vacuous to accommodate the greatness of Maat as a moral form. The most fitting economic form that could work in tandem with Maat is one that is anchored on a solid moral foundation. Maat is precisely that moral foundation, which is yearning for an economic form, particularly relevant for the African condition.

A moral form requires a supportive economic form. Classical Egypt had the right moral form but not the right economic form. Whereas Maat singled out the self as capable of stepping out of its ego shell and embracing other egos outside of it, the corresponding famine and hunger situations forced the actual Egyptian not to embrace the other, but to destroy other selves. It is these particular moments of despair and anguish that killed the enabling moments of patience, justice and love, Maat's feminized principles. The Egyptian self was thus denuded of its potential grandeur, which would make many Afrocentrists, intent on proving the moral superiority of the African self, cry in despair. To say that material deprivation produced moral deprivation is not to argue that at no point did the African self ever present itself as moral. The idealized attempts by Egypt's leaders that led to internalize the limiting conditions of Maat proves the Afrocentric hypotheses that there was a particularly Egyptianized/Africanized effort at internalizing moral greatness, but it was not institutionalized in Egyptian life, the way that the capitalist form did in the 17th century and beyond.

The moral form of life that Maat promised remained on paper, as nothing more than an ideal. The ideals were not institutionalized as ideas, which can be lived, which can be practiced. African thinkers did not take the time to embody these ideals in the life blood of institutions. In short the moral form did not produce a corresponding economic form, in the precise way that the capitalist form produced a corresponding moral form, and institutionalized the latter in far-reaching institutions of the state and its civil society. That is the task that I should like to impose on myself. The celebrated moral features of Maat are generosity, justice, uprightness, tolerance and loving patience. Indeed, these are demanding virtues that capitalism as the dominant economic form cannot support, no matter how diligently it tries.

Adam Smith (1723-1790), the world-famous economist, who was also a moral philosopher, argued that unless capitalism is restrained by morality, as a limiting condition of greed and superfluity, it will eat itself up. To that effect, he developed an elaborate moral theory comprising what he called "moral sentiments" to control the excesses of the market. He proposed compassion and sociality as two powerful moral sentiments that could regulate the excesses of the market. The moral sentiment, he thought, could counter the purely instrumental features of the capitalist economic form. Of course, to this day, his warning of an inevitable doom has yet to be heeded, and capitalism itself continues to marvel at its resiliency to create crises and immediately correct them, thereby proving its "naturalness" and making it easy for its proponents to present it to the world as a God-chosen economic form. Any attempt to counter it with something like Maat is dismissed as a pipe dream. No one in their right mind is expected to take Maat seriously. And the fact that the geographical origin of Maat is an African civilization conveniently results in dismissing Maat as irrelevant and wishful thinking.

Maat as a moral form is considerably deeper than the passing moral sentiments that the Scottish moral philosopher David Hume proposed. Generosity, justice, uprightness, tolerance, wisdom and loving patience go directly against our natural proclivity of injustice, dishonesty, intolerance, closedmindedness, ignorance and hate. These vices seem to fit the ready-to-hand tapestry of our makeup, which by now has become so second nature that no Maat is going to dissemble these powerful vices, which were effectively used to build empires and economic forms that support the visions of the rich and powerful. In contemporary life, revitalizing the features of Maat requires nothing less than manufacturing a new human being.

We must create new human beings, human beings who have to be willing and capable of acting generously, patiently, tolerantly and lovingly. We do not have such human beings in sufficient numbers that matter to construct an economic form that values justice, uprightness, wisdom, tolerance and loving patience. Taking the virtues singly, the following picture emerges. Let us begin with generosity. *Generosity* is a virtue. It is a virtue that is willing to give without receiving, or is willing to give without the deliberate intent of receiving anything, or that the receiving is only an accident, and not an intentional act. The generous person then gives a particular good A to person B; and person B does not simply receive A as a matter of course. B receives A with a profound respect of the giver, and even plans, if she can, to one day reciprocate not in the same way, but in some way. The reciprocity need not be of equal goods. A and B need not be two equal goods, in which equality is measured by money. What makes the act morally compelling is the desire to reciprocate, and not the quantity of the reciprocity.

One of the economic forms of Maat, as illustrated above, is a vision of the self as generous, and generosity itself does not require a calculated practice of reciprocity but simply the desire and the commitment to give when one can, and sometimes to give A to B, although A has to sacrifice good C for the sake of giving A to B, even when one cannot, and perhaps should not, and yet the generous gives nevertheless. One of the central pillars of Maat as an economic form is the cultivation of a human self willing and capable of acting generously in the relational moral regime of giving and receiving, or simply giving without receiving, or receiving with a profound sense of gratitude and respect.

Justice is one of the features of Maat and it is also a potential source of a moral economy, appropriate for the African condition. As Aristotle taught, one does not become just merely by abstractly knowing what justice is; rather, one becomes just by doing just things. The puzzling question is this: if one does not know what justice is then how can she know what just things are, so that she could choose only just things and not others? The question is not easy to answer. But an example might give us a sense of what Aristotle means, and then proceed to discuss the matter at hand: justice as one of the economic forms of Maat.

It is Christmas evening. A family is gathering for a dinner and the table has been set for ten people. Among the popular dishes are five pies, and shortly before the guests arrive, one of the family members has been asked to cut the pies into exact sizes, such that no single person would feel that he has mistakenly picked one of the smallest pies.

The task of the pie cutter is to observe that justice is served and that all the pies are cut evenly and fairly. This is of course an exceedingly difficult task, but justice demands it, and the just cutter must prove the worthiness of her moral action. What must this person do? That is the moral question. Well, at the minimum the person herself must be just in order to perform just action, and in this instance, justice means nothing more than cutting the pieces equally to one's best ability, and that she must do so fairly.

She must cut the pies with a moral imagination and an intuitive mathematical precision, and must pray to the transcendental to make her see justly, and that she is enabled to measure precisely. There is a spiritual dimension to the science of measurement, which could have been simply done with a measuring tape. That possibility, however convenient, is not elegant. She is not going to stand there with a tape or ruler to cut pies. Rather, the expectations are two, that (1) she is going to make an effort to be precise, because her intention is to be just and (2) that her eyes are just, or that she prays that they would be. (1) and (2) are the requirements; the rest is left to moral imagination.

She cuts the pies, and it turns out that all the pieces appear to be equal, and when the guests arrive, they randomly pick the pieces, and appear to be clearly satisfied. What we have here is a display of justice in the Aristotelian sense, in which justice is defined as an activity that is guided by a measure of equality, and equality itself is manifest in the attempt at being fair to everyone, and in this example, an attempt to be fair to the guests, without their ever knowing that they are being worked on. They judge the event as illuminated by justice, and the event as uplifting. They eat, drink, converse, dance and leave.

Justice presents itself in this event, through the presence of those delicious pies, each of which is a duplicate of the other. Generalizing this to a higher level, what we can say is that any economic form must be guided with justice as an event of doing things fairly and that all the commodities that human beings should want must be distributed with such a standard, the standard of justice as fairness. Given justice as fairness, commodity A can be distributed between persons B and C in such an equitable way that B and C share commodity A by getting the same amount at any time, any place and for a good reason.

Compassion is another feature of Maat; indeed, it is one of the cardinal moral forms for the new moral economy that I am theorizing here. Compassion is to moral economy as greed is to capitalism. One cannot imagine capitalism without the salient principle of greed, and similarly, one cannot imagine moral economy without the original principle of compassion. The modern world is divided by class, race, gender, ethnicity and groups. Out of these divisions it is class division that is the most decisive, as it is also the one that seems to be so natural that we cannot surmount the pain and agony that it produces. In a class-divided world, compassion is the least present, because there is no compelling reason that persuades individuals to be compassionate if they are not naturally compassionate, or are inclined toward it. Of course, where compassion is not naturally present, it could be taught either by example or directly through teaching.

An example should elucidate the place of compassion in moral economy. It is summer, and exhaustingly hot. People that you encounter are hot tempered too. Everybody is on edge, including yourself. You happen to be a coffee lover, so there you are standing behind a long line of people to get your fix. The heat has made you really impatient, and you are ready to explode on anything around you. You are also naturally generous but not this day. Soon, before you leave the coffee shop, a homeless person smiles at you and tries to engage you in a conversation, hoping that you will understand the purpose of the conversation. Of course you understand, but you ignore him and walk by. But then something bothers you, and you come back to the coffee shop and generously give the man what he wanted. You are proud of yourself, because you have done what generosity demands, that you control your temper and perform the morally correct action. Surely, you say to yourself, it was not easy, but you did it.

Now you wonder what all this means, and why you did it. It is obvious to you why you did the action. Indeed, it is because you are really a compassionate human being but also a religious person. You really have no obligation to pay attention to that person. He is not related to you, he is not an ex-friend that fortune turned against, nor did you do it so as to be a hero by the media.

Your action is morally worthy only because you have internalized compassion. To you compassion comes quite naturally. It is part of your moral frame. Any repeated action becomes a habit. So compassionate action comes habitually to you. You rarely fight it. Rather, you exuberantly let it lead your way, as it eventually did on that hot and difficult day. But even on that day you conquered the temptation of doubt, and excessive self love, by the moral force of compassion. That is why you corrected yourself, when you were briefly but powerfully tempted by forgetfulness on that hot day and returned to do the morally right thing.

Compassion is morally compelling when it is extended to a total other, which has nothing to do with our lives, other than the silent duty we have toward those who await our moral attention. It is much easier to be compassionate toward a loved one, a friend, a relative and even an acquaintance; harder is the task when the subject is a real other, such as that homeless person by the coffee shop. In order for any action to be morally worthy the motive must be pure, and the purity is measured by the quality and quantity of the compassion that is extended to any needy human being, uncontaminated by external motives, such as love, friendship, acquaintance and relation.

It is in this particular way that I am arguing that compassion serves Maat. *Tolerance* is a crucial feature of moral economy. In fact, it could easily be argued that it is an indispensable organizing principle, which works in tandem with loving kindness. Just as we cannot love a person without respecting her, except delusorily, we cannot live with one another without tolerating each others' needs, habits, likes and dislikes.

In the economic sphere tolerance is subtly pertinent. We cannot readily sense its inner working unless we pay attention to its musings at the workplace, as we interact with one another as bosses and employees.

Consider the following example to underscore the point. There is this employee who does things in ways that many people find annoying. She customarily comes late to work; she procrastinates; she spreads papers, cans and foodstuffs all around her–sometimes she cannot even find herself amid the dirt, the pile and the dust. Yet, and this is the point, whatever she does is done flawlessly, as flawless as human products could be. Her boss has agonized over what to do with her; he has contemplated firing her numerous times. Lulled by the elegance of her work and his loving-kindness toward her, he decides to keep her. He has promised himself to erase those occasional thoughts of getting rid of her. As he told one of his friends, he has learned, and not very easily, the ways of tolerance as a principle of management, of managing employees who will not and cannot change their habits for the rest of their lives.

I consider this manager very wise and skilled at the art of management. He decided, obviously, because he could change himself as hard as it was, rather than expect his employee to change. The structure of his thoughts could be put syllogistically:

Y can change his way
X cannot change easily
Therefore Y must change for the sake of Z.

Y is the manager. X is the annoying employee. Z is the organization where Y and X work. In this situation Z is saved precisely because the manager internalizes tolerance and loving-kindness as the organizing principles of the organization. Y controls his ego and chooses to advance the interests of Z over and against his own private needs. He does not fire X because his ego demands it. Nor does he ever insist that X must change. He has intuitively and empirically concluded that it is pointless to expect X to change, nor would it benefit Z to lose X, since X is an intelligent and skilled worker.

Where tolerance is habitually practiced at workplaces it becomes an indispensable good that could save many employers the unnecessary cost that is incurred on hiring and firing employees and ease the distress of the families and loved ones of employers and employees. Tolerance can easily remedy the situation. If it is much easier for managers to change than it is for excellent employees with annoying habits, and then it is those who can change their ways who must change for the sake of a functional and democratic moral economy.

FROM

Dekilula.com, August 9, 2006.

SOURCE

Adam Smith, *The Theory of Moral Sentiments*, (1759*)*.

35

AN ECONOMIC FORM FOR AFRICA

Patience is a feature of Maat. The ideal leader as well as the ideal citizen must patiently wait to witness the appearance of the transcendent. Nothing great is accomplished without a transcendental intervention, the seal of completeness, of generosity and justice, two other features of moral economy, as I have argued in the previous essay.

Rarely is patience, however, associated with economic forms. Economic forms are founded on seizing the opportunity before it vanishes. The activity is everything but patient. Patience and quick money making are the virtues of capitalism. In that world view, success is measured by shrewdness, quickness, impatience and opportunism. Whereas patience is undermined by capitalism, the economic form for Maat reveres it. The economic form for the African condition demands it. Without this virtue the disadvantaged citizen of the African continent is doomed, fated to starve and die.

A moral economy, in contrast, when founded on Maat, shares with Maat an ardent belief in patient waiting, and this is particularly true during times of famine, poverty and loss. Patient waiting is the much-needed virtue that both generosity and justice demand. An example might illuminate the abstraction.

African economy in country A has been blooming, and the Western world has been hailing it as a model for the future. Country A gets spoiled and its inhabitants shop madly. No commodity is beyond their reach, so they think. Suddenly, all things, with the exception of the transcendent, change, since no condition is permanent. The oil fields drain. The spoils of the economy are distributed unevenly.

The citizens become impatient with country A, which had introduced them to the pangs of luxury, which have now become the pangs of hunger. Friends turn against friends. The shopping frenzy slows down. Their lovers do not love the men anymore. The rate of divorce increases, since the men's ability to maintain expensive lifestyles are no more.

Patient waiting for better days is not a norm. Loves and friendships founded on comfort, wealth and excessive wealth are not permanent. They flounder as easily as they initially sprawled. Things that last must be built slowly, in the furnace of time, and be sculpted in accordance with the laws of beauty.

Country A is no longer a model of hope, but a model of despair. An economic form that does not institutionalize patient waiting as a way of life digs its grave when conditions change. That is why patient waiting also must be systematically insinuated in the African citizen's psyche, as an ethics of living, and a stylistics of what I have previously called existential seriousness. A responsible economic form must inculcate the virtue of patience among its citizens, from early on. This complicated and demanding virtue must be taught at all levels of school. It must be part of economic principles, and be taught as such, and not be pushed to the sidelines, as part of religion and theology, which does not have much to do with morals, and has nothing to do with economics. It is this dogma of capitalist economics, that must change.

My argument here is a modest contribution to challenge one of the foundational dogmas of bourgeois economics. The morals must guide economics and a new moral economy that works in concert with moral philosophy and religion is precisely what the African condition requires. More morality, with a distinct religious voice, such as the notion of patient waiting, will strengthen and expand our horizons as we struggle with poverty, famine and other sorrows of modern life.

We need more people who can patiently wait as everything changes, hopeful that no condition is permanent, including the conditions of nations, when their economies get distorted and the citizens are hardened and become cruel toward one another, and the notion of helping your fellow citizens sounds indeed very strange to those who are comfortable. Instead, during trying times, citizens do not patiently wait for things to change; instead, they give up altogether, or become irreligious and immoral. It is in this way that patient waiting, I argue, becomes one of the pillars of moral economy, one of the features of Maat, along with generosity and justice.

From

Dekialula.com, August 9, 2006.

36

THE AFRICANIZATION OF FAMINE

Classical Egypt illustrated very deeply what famines can do to the human psyche in a dramatic way. When Egypt was hit by a devastating famine, the true colors of human beings under duress was uncovered for all to see. Humans literally ate other human beings; home regimes were looted mercilessly; neighbors killed neighbors for survival. "Desperate times call for desperate measures" is a saying that aptly applied to the human condition in Classical Egypt.

The moral intelligence that I have been repeatedly invoking did not furnish its services to the ancient Egyptians during times of despair. The direct opposite of moral intelligence, namely, cruelty, was forced on the Egyptian victims of famine.

What was true then could also assert itself once more on home regimes and civil society's regimes unless great caution is taken against the ten-year cycle of famines that rampage the East African landscape, and that is now extending itself to the rest of Africa. Suffering does not necessarily produce sensitive human beings; on the contrary, suffering could easily produce resentful, spiteful and angry human beings intent on inflicting suffering on others.

For example, Dostoyevsky's underground man, in *Notes from Underground*, specialized in inflicting pain on himself and on others out of spite, and enjoyed it.

Famines in particular and poverty in general do set human beings against one another, instead of overcoming their pains by the resources of counterhegemonic practices of compassion, care and generosity. We cannot bring out the best of Africans until they are freed from the pangs of hunger and the barbarity of famines through a combination of collective political action, to be undertaken by the victims themselves and effective public policies.

The collective political action must be linked to the organizing of social movements out of the resources of civil society and its various regimes at the workplace, churches, social clubs, once the foundational work of character development is done at the home regimes, through indispensable work of mothers and fathers.

From

Dekialula.com, March 15, 2006.

Source

Fyodor Dosteyevsky, *Notes from Underground & The Grand Inquisitor*, New York: E.P. Dutton & Co., Inc., 1960.

37

THE LANGUAGE OF FAMINE

All human practices have languages of their own. Laughter is the language of joy; irony is the language of ambiguity; crying is the language of joy and sadness. Famine too has its own peculiar language. Cruelty is that rare language of famine that has presenced itself in the interstices of classical Egypt as I argued in essay no. 62, "The Africanization of Famine." The horrors of famine forced humans in classical Egypt, during the seven years of famine, to reveal to the world the essence of their being, an essence not grounded on the biological constitutions of their being, about which we know very little, but rather on the conditions of deprivation that lasted seven long years, and finally changed the very nature of their Egyptianess, the chief features of which were courage, spiritedness and contagious elegance of manners and polish. The seven years of suffering produced a totally different sense of Africanity, manifest in the way they treated each other, through horrendous cruelties of eating other human beings, killing their neighbors. Long was the grounding of their humanity on the organizing principle of Matt, a symbol of uprightness, compassion, analytic acuity, penetrating wisdom and justice.

The inclusive and transformative language of Matt was replaced by the prejudiced and closed language of cruelty, consecrated during the period of famine. The new self of Egyptianess was fortified during those seven long years of famine, which must have given reason to Thomas Hobbes in the 17th century to have the most pessimistic vision of human nature, as nasty, short and brutish. That was exactly how classical Egypt presented itself during the seven bad years of famine.

FROM

Dekialula.com, July 19, 2006.

38

COUNTERHEGEMONY

Counterhegemony enables the deeply disempowered African masses to take hold of their destinies by determining their future life chances with courage and strategic planning. Their existential seriousness shows them their future paths in concert with the transcendent's presence. Nothing great is accomplished without God's blessings. However, we cannot and should not burden this generous and life-giving God with responsibilities that we must shoulder. Fighting famine and hunger in the end is our human responsibility. God has given us natural resources for our use but we must use these resources intelligently and responsibly.

Whereas the hegemons try to convince us famines and hungers are forces we cannot control without the help of the rich and powerful Caucasians, counterhegemonic thoughts show us the ways by which we can control the controllable and resign to forces outside of our inherent capacity to control. Change begins with the realization that there are things that are in the sphere of our control and things that are outside of that sphere of control. The hegemons do not only confuse these two spheres but mystify the causes of our suffering. Again it is us, Africans, who should not only know the crucial differences, but also it is us who must map out what we must do to change our destinies.

Our destinies are always in our hands, and how to effect the needed change requires nothing short of fundamentally revolutionizing our value and work ethics. We must create new values and ethics that empower, affirm and teach us the way of self-reliance within the intimate spheres of our homes, our schools, our neighborhoods, our work places, our communities, our regions and, finally, our continent.

FROM

Dekialula.com, May 25, 2006.

3 9

THE VOICES OF COUNTERHEGEMONY

W omen sitting on dark corners in the dawn nursing tending onions and moist tomatoes to feed a family of ten; priests chanting at churches and begging God not to forsake the famished and the hungry; teenagers hanging out at street corners ready to accept any leftovers; the rich and powerful spoiling themselves with drinks and food that the poorest of the poor can only dream about; prostitutes selling themselves to anyone and for anything available. These are the scenes produced by hegemonic ideology on behalf of the rich and powerful, and which the emerging voices of counterhegemony seek to change.

Long after famines are temporarily averted by the monies thrown at us Ethiopians and others by the famine-fatigued Western world, they leave behind huge piles of poverty and squalor in the shantytowns of Addis and other Ethiopian cities. By the time that famines leave the scene, hunger and poverty immediately take over, and they naturalize themselves to our tired eyes. The massive poverty that presses on Ethiopian lives is taken for granted. We Ethiopians have been assuming for years that poverty is distinctly Ethiopian. Indeed our literature has long treated poverty as part of Ethiopian poetics, which cannot be changed. Our tragedies are mediated through the poetics of poverty, and our songs are watered by the lives of the poor. We sing about them.

The poor have become an integral part of Ethiopian visual treasure. We see the poor without really seeing them; we listen to the poor without listening to them. The poor have entered our homes as commodities we can discard. They are not beings with rights but nonbeings born to suffer. In the interiors of our villas, the poor maids are our dumping grounds. We abuse them, we intimidate them, we hire and fire them and we rape them.

It is these alienated voices of counterhegemony who must speak, who must protest and who must organize to change their conditions and wake us up from the slumbers of our deep sleep.

From

Dekialula.com, May 25, 2006.

40

INTRODUCING A COUNTERHEGEMONIC VISION

By counterhegemony, I mean a sustained attempt at overthrowing ideas, values and programmes that are imposed on the governed without either their critical understanding or their consent. The idea that famines and hungers are caused by forces beyond the control of the governed is opposed by counterhegemony as a deeply flawed idea that must be resisted by any means necessary, including armed resistance. To say that famine is caused by nature is only half of the truth, even that half truth can be overcome by the forces of technology, if the governed have the means by which to develop the technologies appropriate to the African situation.

The artificial causes of nature on the other hand are products of an ideology that masquerades as truth and mystifies the process by which famines are created, sustained and justified. It is precisely these mystifications that counterhegemony effectively exposes, so that the governed can participate in the constructions of realities that fulfill their dreams and hopes. Counterhegemony empowers and enables the governed to independently create self-reliant institutions that promote the African condition.

The next essay will analyze the relationships between counterhegemony and the famine and hunger regimes in contemporary Africa.

FROM
Dekialula.com, May 17, 2006.

41

HEGEMONY AND FAMINE

By hegemony, I mean a modality of ruling and dominating the masses by (a) the force of unthought-out ideas and (b) by the use of violence and the threat of using violence by way of intimidating the masses. Hegemony then is a method that power holders use in the systematic dissemination of their world view, on those whom they seek to govern. Books, magazines, sermons, clubs and many other tools of the state and civil society are employed in the systematic spread of the core values of the dominant group, which in turn produce some docile citizens, citizens who do not question what is handed to them, citizens who believe without contesting, subjects who consent without understanding. Not all of them of course, since there will always be critical, skeptical and courageous individuals who refuse to believe without understanding. Docility and apparent obedience are intended features of subjects, who are not citizens, that the hegemons sculpt in the first and the third worlds; in the first world citizens are trained not to think critically, and in the third world they are socialized to submit to their faith of living with famines, hunger and squalor. Africa is a prime victim of this intricate process of brainwashing and disempowering.

Hegemony is diffused both through the spread of dominant ideas and through violence and the threat of the use of violence. The state plays a key role in the actual use of violence, when citizens either disobey or openly revolt. In our time, as we recently witnessed in Iraq and Ethiopia and as we continue to observe in the interiors of the civil societies of many other nations, citizens and subjects are being governed by hegemonic tools of subtle socialization and by imprisonment and invasions.

The artificial causes of famine are classic paradigms of hegemoically engineered modalities of beliefs, which are diffused throughout capitalist and socialist states by way of silencing the voices of autonomous citizens against their best judgments. They are taught to believe in falsehoods, so that they would not revolt against their exploiters. So daring are the hegemons that they even use religion to convince the victims of famine that famine is caused by natural forces, thereby remaining oblivious to the artificial causes of famine, causes that could be changed by critical revolutionary action, a moment of counterhegemony.

This hegemonic view is pushed against reflective citizens and this in spite of the resistance of some of the most enlightened members of modern society in historic nations, such as Ethiopia. Some of the masses know rather well that famine and hunger have both natural and artificial reasons, and yet the hegemons force them to think otherwise; if they dare to resist hegemony they draw their swords against unarmed citizens. So the masses, seriously anchored to existence, acquiesce to their deplorable condition. By this means the indifferent state in Africa and elsewhere continues to conflate and confound the vigilant masses by cloaking artificial reasons with the mystifying garment of external nature.

FROM

Dekialula.com, May 7, 2006.

42

FAMINE AND THE ORGANIZATION OF THE SELF

Indeed, the self is distinguished by the capacity of organizing its moral life. What is true of the self as such is also true of the African self. The moral organization of the self is a universal project. All world cultures have organizing principles. Africans also have crafted over their vast history particular ways of organizing their moral life.

Moral life is manifest in the way we make a living, most evident in our work habits, our priorities, our food intake, our sense of time and our sensitivity to space, to history and to the presence of others. When measured by these yardsticks, Africans have done exceedingly well. The way various African cultures treat the elderly, respond to the suffering of others, the depth and frequency of their generosities present Africans to the world as extremely civilized.

Hegemonic ideologies, however, minimize the significance of these moral virtues and ridicule them as recipes of disaster. African generosity is contrasted with the instrumental work ethic of capitalism and found to be wanting and primitive.

Generosity to a total stranger, which is a frequent African value, is not foolish. In fact, it is the ultimate expression of unconditional kindness, for which Africans should be praised. That this value is not praised does not connote a failure of reason but rather reveals those who cannot glorify this disinterested measure of morality as morally uncivilized. It is too easy to be kind to a loved one, to a family member, to a friend, but extremely difficult to be kind to a total stranger on the street. A disinterested moral action is at it very best when it is exercised without any motive and result but purely and simply as the profoundest exercise of moral intelligence.

FROM

Dekialula.com, April 14, 2006.

43

FAMINE AND MORAL ORGANIZATION

Consider the follow...   many people.
Famine ...   ...ote a subtlety
he...   ...be fed, and
wh...   ...too many of
ther...   ...e are scarce
good...   ...nite goods
in thi...   ...overpopu-
lation...   ...nevitably
becom...   ...oposedly
burden...   ...the fact
of scarc...   ...tion of
another i...   ...in the
following...   ...aving
too many...   ...l and
uncultured...

Poor pe...   ...they bred
like flies an...   ...nite goods. If poor
people knew...   ...their lives, they would know precisely how to p...—...themselves against the ravishes of famine by
having fewer children, substantial savings, good work habits and
functional values. Poverty by definition, the Malthusians think,
is a function of moral disorganization. Poor people contribute to
the misery of the world by their irresponsibilities and inability to
control their destinies.

Moral disorganization propelled by dysfunctional values is
antithetical to war against poverty. In his time, Malthus protested
against the existence of poor people and suggested their slow
death, so that the world could plan intelligently by assuming scar-
city as a feature of the human condition. None of these arguments
are true. For years, however, humanity has been feasting on them

as truths, which have insinuated themselves into our thinking lives as ideologies. It is outrageously propagated that poor people do not plan, are lascivious, suffer from the victimization syndrome, eat badly, undernourish themselves and much else. I call this way of framing moral knowledge hegemonic ideologies.

FROM

Dekialula.com, April 14, 2006.

44

FAMINE AND CULTURE

Culture is a way of organizing a life and giving oneself a life chance. A life chance is an organization of a future. Although life is very short, we can make it enjoyable and bearable by organizing our short lives in such a way that the misery is less and the mishaps are controllable. When our lives are marred by famine, hunger and poverty our future is put in jeopardy and our lives are encumbered by sorrow and profound depression, natural facts that orchestrate themselves when our emaciated and shamed bodies are exposed to an indifferent world. One of the central ways by which we can control our life chances, and therefore our future, is to organize.

Culture is precisely that organizing device, which works with and against nature. It works with nature, when nature favors us with its charms and graces. A genetically endowed person is so favored by nature that all that she has to do is use the genetic gift and use culture to organize it, to be the best athlete, the best dancer or the best thinker.

Culture combats nature when the African self is not endowed, and therefore not favored by nature. Then Africa works even harder to culturally organize herself, so that she can construct herself against external nature, against the given, against all that is outside of our control.

When Africans are hit hard, harder than other population groups, it is incumbent on them to work creatively and control their life chances to the extent that they can. It is at this level of intervention that Africans must think and fight hard to resist the whims of nature. Droughts, as I have argued, are bound to hit African soil anytime, to any degree and for a determined natural reason. We Africans must expect that fact, and we must culturally organize ourselves to fight back with the resources of our intelligence, resilience and faith.

Culture is precisely that device that we use to organize our moral lives. Our moral lives are expressions of values we cherish. Hard work, discipline and honesty are among the values that we hold dear. The availability of these values and many others like them are the cultural devices we use to fight back when famines strike us.

FROM

Dekialula.com, April 6, 2006.

45

THE CAUSES OF FAMINE (PART 1)

Drought is one of the causes of famine. Natural disasters of all kinds have afflicted humankind for millennia. The Torah introduces us most poignantly to the disastrous famine that afflicted a record number of desperate Egyptian bodies for seven years. The fat years of plenty and prosperity were replaced by seven lean years of anguish, famine and desperation. In time, through the miraculous transcendental intervention, the lean years were displaced by the fat years. This was a classic locus of time and patience healing the wounds of an ancient African civilization.

The plagues of locusts are also another major source of famine. This natural phenomenon has been systematically contained by modern science in Europe and elsewhere in the materially civilized world; whereas Africa continues to be ravished by locust infestation to this very day. One of the devastating consequences of natural famines is population reduction. China in 1867-1868 under the Tonghi Restoration was afflicted by famine, and the province of Shanxi was depopulated substantially. An estimated mortality of 9.5-13 million people occurred.

African famines are also exasperated by natural facts peculiar to the continent, such as that African soils are made up of sand and laterite, which erode easily and hold less water, even where there is plenty of rain, than the clayey and humus regions of vast portions of the world. The high iron and aluminum content makes the African soil systems hard to turn, therefore less exposed to sun and air, which in turn results in noncultivatable land. Thus African soil systems become devegetated and turn into dry land, which cannot absorb rain. At the end of these tragic facts, drought appears as the final kiss of death, and famine is the expected result.

FROM

Dekialula.com, March 15, 2006.

46

THE CAUSES OF FAMINE (PART 2)

Famine is caused by several factors. There are natural and artificial reasons. Drought is a natural cause. War, shortage of food, mismanaged resources and population growth are artificial causes. As the previous essay addressed the natural causes of famine extensively, I will now move on to consider the role of politics, culture and behavior in the production of famine, as instances of the artificial causes of famine.

Leading experts in the world have identified drought and crop failure as the leading forces behind famine. The natural causes of famine are beyond our control. Science, however, can help us to mitigate the role of nature in making us helpless. We can, for example, improve the means of transportation by making it possible for a "rich harvest" in one site to supplement a poor harvest in another area. Of course no matter what we do, we cannot control the devastating power of hail, storm, frost and the like. We can, however, do as the French did in Algiers to combat locust infestation. Effective water storage systems can also avert the impact of famine. Local and regional famines in our time are directly caused by natural causes. The chief causes are the inability to regulate the patterns of rainfall, the ineffectiveness of systems of water storage and the complications of enhancing the infertility of dry lands. These are some of the main natural causes of famine, which the West has already combated with improved scientific measures, whereas Africa continues to be plagued by them.

Natural causes produced some of the major famines in the world. There was a great famine in Egypt; the great famine in Rome in 436 B.C.; the great famine in India between 1790-1792 that killed so many people that they could not even be buried properly; in 1846-1847 famine in Ireland killed hundreds of people; the famine in Russia in 1891-1892; the famine of 1887-

1889 in China. These are some of the major parts of the world that have experienced famine.

In all these regions famines are directly caused by the forces of nature beyond human control, and yet major scientific efforts were made to prepare against the expected arrival of famines. India in particular did not successfully combat the natural causes, because it did not have functional democratic institutions guided by effective public policies well into the twentieth century.

From

Dekialula.com, April 3, 2006.

47

FAMINE AND PERSONHOOD

When famine strikes, the self loses a very important right, the right to a future. Put in a syllogistic form, the argument looks like this: Famine is the absence of a right to an X. Y is famished. Therefore, Y loses X.

X is a right to a future, no matter what that future is. Y is that person who is famished and is therefore automatically denied an important right to a future life. That future is precisely the right that is denied to those entire Ys who die from famine. Those who deny these futures do so with the arrogant belief that the African future is already known, that it is bleak, hopeless and as predictable as the fact that there will always be a new day. They therefore reckon that there is no future to speak of, since that future is already determined absent, when it is applied to the African condition. That they are wrong is obvious, but that wrongness needs to be elucidated.

I should now like to explicate the above syllogism, by applying it to the human condition in Africa. At any time that famine strikes any part of the continent, the continent is denuded of millions of human beings, each of whom symbolizes a life with a future; it is irrelevant what that future may be. Only those who do not wish Africans well deduce from the fact that the continent is poor that the future will also be poor. This argument is simply wrong, not to say that it is callous, unseemly, indecent and ill-mannered. It predicts the future of the unborn by premising that future life on the lives of those who have been made poor by hegemonic institutions.

The syllogism of the argument is thus: Africans are generally poor. Famished Africans are beyond poverty. If they survive famine they would still remain permanently hungry and poor. This syllogism is not only callously formulated but hides deep indifference if not outright racism toward dark-skinned human beings in Africa and its Diasporas. We all know that it is European colonialism and

American racism that planted the seeds of destitution in African lands. Seventy-five years of colonialism and an ongoing systematic racism continue to haunt the African presence everywhere. The remnants of exploitation of African land have left their marks on every facet of modern African life. Education, health, work (if ever available) are affected by the marks of slavery in the American soil and the blend of colonialism and slavery in the African soil and its Diasporas, and yet the syllogism above hides these facts and cavalierly states lies and an incredible denial of historical facts.

Unless these facts are directly faced as the ultimate explanations of the African present condition, then famine and hunger will remain as mysteries that defy reasonable and rational explanations, which we ought to extract first from history and then from the habits and ethos of African culture. The second syllogism rejects historical facts and resorts to analytic statements violently divorced from the ways in which history has produced the present African reality. This reality is that Africa simply does not have the material resources with which to contain the natural calamities of famine. When famine strikes in the African soil it destroys African capital, primarily human beings with a future, their cattle and other crucial resources of labor power. Famine and hunger are inextricably intertwined. In the African condition in particular, they are intimately interconnected, as I will demonstrate.

FROM

Dekialula.com, March 6, 2006.

48

FAMINE: THE LANGUAGE OF AFRICAN TRAGEDY

The specter of famine is once again haunting the East African landscape. Soon the reluctant world is going to be visited by African faces enshrouded by impending death in the hands of time flying on the wings of hunger. Many East African faces, young and old, male and female, are going to flood global television with their emaciated bodies, thinned out faces, helplessly looking at us the viewers, when we are nursing our caramel macchiato in a pleasant coffee house and bloating ourselves with our delicious Ethiopian dishes, and fighting out our politics.

Well, that is not going to be the case. Soon nature will compel us to visit our hearts and care for our dying brothers and sisters who will soon stare at us through their eyes struck by grief and sunken by hunger. For now all my attempts to create the mood for political love through the reconciliatory power of pure reason guided by the imperatives of the transcendent will be put on hold, as the human condition in East Africa places the burden of thinking for my brothers and sisters on my shaking shoulders, and I demand that every Ethiopian makes an effort to organize national chapters, for what I would like to call The Famine and Hunger Project with a Pan-African orientation and a continental vision.

If we care enough about our brothers and sisters in the Horn of Africa, we would soon make a determined effort to save any amount of money and put it in the treasury of our local chapters of The Famine project. We must put aside for now our important political differences and save our brothers and sisters from gazing at Western television and begging for food, when we ourselves could travel miles with our hard-earned wages in the West and share portions of them with those who desperately need them.

Now is the time to suspend our political fights and make concerted national efforts to raise millions of dollars and help out the victims.

It is either now or never. Not to act now is irresponsible. To act now is not only responsible but a moral obligation, commanded by the moral law inside every Ethiopian heart. Let us visit our hearts and be the best Ethiopians we can be.

This short essay merely introduces The Famine and Hunger Project that will remain active as long as the famine persists. Future essays will analyze the impending peril of famine under the name of The Famine and Hunger Project. I invite my readers to wish me well in this most important project.

FROM

Dekialula.com, March 6, 2006.

49

FAMINE, HUNGER AND PUBLIC ACTION: MODEST POLICY PROPOSALS FOR ETHIOPIA

The specter of pessimism continues to haunt discussions of famine and hunger in sub-Saharan Africa. However, this pessimism is misplaced and missituated—because famines and hunger everywhere in the world can be overcome, by systematic public action. The brilliant Amartya Sen, the Nobel Laureate for Economics in 1998, has devoted his life to the study of famines, and has recently written, "One of the problems that makes the task of the prevention of famines and hunger particularly difficult is the general sense of pessimism and defeatism that characterizes so much of the discussions of poverty and hunger in the modern world. While pictures of misery and starvation arouse sympathy and pity across the world, it is often taken for granted that nothing much can be done to remedy these desperate situations, at least in the short run (Tanco Memorial Lecture, August 1990).

These subtle words apply to the recurrence of famine and perpetual hunger in Ethiopia with unprecedented urgency. If you asked any Ethiopian legislator why famines occur with such consistency, he might look at you in surprise and reply that it is a natural mishap manifest in crop failure, and the sluggishness and cursed existence of the victims. Of course, some of our ardent critical revolutionaries seek to advance what they call structural explanations. The latter explanation is the correct one.

Famine can be immediately curtailed if legislators make sure that peasant laborers, such as the Ethiopian nomads of the south, are not forced by desperation during periods of famine to consume their animals instead of preserving them for the creation of value, by seeing to it they are always helped by an efficient state to possess the necessary purchasing power to buy food where it is available, without eating their potentially value-creating animals. It is the duty of the state to feed, clothe and house the victims of famine. Similarly, those fortunate producers who have the food grains that the famished need should be forced by public action not to engage in speculative withdrawals and panic hoarding, thereby contributing to the desperation of the hungry and endemically deprived.

During periods of famine and immediately after, primary producers of food should be encouraged to export grains if they are so able. The state must create the appropriate market for them so that they can slowly begin to get purchasing power and live productive lives again. If they can, they too are entitled to purchase luxury goods like the consumers of the city. They need not necessarily suffer from envy and jealousy, and harbor deep resentments of the city dweller. Envy and jealousy propel many ethnic conflicts. Systematic public action can remove this destructive state of mind. The peasant and the city dweller can work toward a common good.

As in Bengal in 1943, in which 3 million people died, a majority of which were fishermen, transport workers and agricultural laborers, in Ethiopia, too, the victims are invariably poor peasants and pastoral nomads. Sen writes, "it is they who eat their animal products directly and also sell animals to buy food grains (thereby making a net gain in calories, on which he is habitually dependent). Similarly, a Bengali fisherman does consume some fish, though for his survival he is dependent on grain calories which he obtains at a favorable calories exchange rate by selling fish—a luxury food for most Bengali" (Amartya Sen, *Poverty and Famines*, p. 951).

The parallels between Ethiopia and Bengal are arresting. Both poor economies are pressured by desperation to make suicidal economic decisions. Both economies behave unproductively, in search of immediate purchasing power in order to exist. Had there been a functional state, it would have intervened and procured the right to eat without squandering crucial economic sources of value creation. Matters become worse. Those who manage to survive famines remerge on the streets of major cities as hungry and permanently poor. Consider the following image of a day in Addis, which I witnessed on Bole road in 1995.

I woke up at one o'clock in the afternoon to a flood of light that the tropical sun gave the city of Addis on a beautiful day in late summer. It was early in the afternoon when I was strolling on a familiar avenue through a deafening crowd. On this busy afternoon, thousands of exhausted people were returning from work; a vendor was pushing his famished young chicken for hard sale; a prostitute was offering her lanky body for the whole night for a quarter; a shoeshine boy was offering his services for a penny; beggars were chanting, surrounded by an admiring crowd; the street cafes were teeming with idlers sharing a pot of tea among ten people; children were pleading for money by aggressively putting their sickly hands inside wealthy people's big cars, and getting whisked away like flies; a preacher in the corner was telling the passersby that unless they mend their selfish ways, they are going to be consumed by a ferocious famine that might erase the inhabitants from the face of the earth; standing directly opposite from the preacher, a politician was campaigning and promising that he will bring prosperity and peace to every citizen. I smiled sadly, when I heard a small boy, "Sir, you are God, since you were chosen to be the wealthiest, so please give me money, it is God's money after all."

I continued strolling down the avenue invaded by sadness. I saw a blind man carrying a deaf old woman, which turned out to be his mother. A passerby had just rudely thrown a coin at him, another dry bread, with which he was feeding his mother, until another younger beggar snatched the bread, to unhappily discover that another one-eyed beggar had just swiftly managed to take away from the previous unlawful owner. A small dog joined the scene longingly eyeing the bones owned by the boy, that it managed to snatch from a little boy, and run away with his catch, rejoicing his success.

A few yards away, a boy, small, nicely built, super black with shiny and semioily skin, nakedly exposing his private parts to whomever had the temptation to see, was annoying the passersby. He was dancing, by running left and right. Some women would secretly glance at him and whisper words to one another. Men would outrightly shout rude words at him, except that he did not care. He had apparently entered a trance. Young children giggled, jumped up and down and, innocently convinced that that the boy was giving them a show, refused their mothers' desperate efforts to save them from cultural poisoning. The boy continued his act.

The harassed strollers and nervous walkers appeared neither shocked nor amused only annoyed. The large avenue was slowly populated by a variety of expensive cars. Behind their wheels sat brightly dressed and overgrown men. These were the wealthy residents of Addis on their way to lavish weddings and parties at the majestic Hilton Hotel. Far away into the end of the avenue, is the palace, which was built by the emperor.

The characters above are the victims of endemic deprivation. Some have migrated from the famished countryside. Some have been festering there for years. No one knows where he or she is born. Few care about when and how they die. Systematic public action is challenged to address their condition.

The economically deprived subjects in Ethiopia, the victims of famines and hunger, are targets of public action—a blend of state action and market activities. In my article "The African Union," I introduced two principles of justice, and proposed that legislators must be guided by principles of justice. The first principle sought to ensure that the hungry must be fully fed, clothed and sheltered as a mater of inalienable human right. Only after that condition is satisfied can irresponsible spending at Ethiopian hotels be given a blind eye.

The members of the media must freely expose and criticize the discrepancy of poverty and wealth. Corruption, lavish spending abroad, endemic poverty at home, uneven purchasing power, the demystification of famines and hunger must be discussed in the public sphere, at Parliament, in the classroom. The public must be informed and its conscience must be haunted. Prostitutes and their parents must be given medical literacy about their violated bodies. In this regard, Ethiopians can learn from the heroic successes of the poor state of Kerala, India, where medical literacy has become a right and life expectancy has been generously extended to seventy years.

Those idle children I described above can be trained at very low cost to participate in the market to help themselves. Ethiopia can learn from South Korea, Hong Kong and Singapore economies of value, which have successfully combined economic expansion with social responsibility to the disadvantaged poor, by reducing infant mortality and illiteracy. As Sen put the matter, "It is not legitimate to wonder whether a poor country can 'afford' to spend so much on health and education that many poor countries (such as Sri Lanka,

China, Costa Rica, the Indian State of Kerala and others) have done precisely that with much success, but also understand the general fact that the cost of delivering public health care and basic education facilities is enormously cheaper in a poor country than in a rich one" (Tanco Memorial Lecture, p. 5).

Finally and most important, legislators must be advised to avoid costly wars that plunder value-creating economies. Peace and prosperity for all must be the goal of the hopeful Ethiopia. Famines and hunger can be eliminated by the actions of a morally sensitive market and systematic public action. Diversification and peace must be the engines of change in a new Ethiopia.

FROM

Walta Information Center, July 23, 2000.

SOURCES

Amarta Sen, Tanco Memorial Lecture, August, 1990; *Poverty and Famines*, Oxford: Clarendon Press, 1982.

Teodros Kiros, "*The African Union*," Walta Information Center, July 23, 2000

50

THE HOME REGIME

Countering oppressive ways of life and making a living begins at home; hence the analysis of the home regime is a crucial component of counterhegemonic possibilities. It is not an accident that the Greek philosopher Aristotle considered home to be the center of economic activities as well as the site of civil society, which is run by women, as the economists of the household, and who inculcate formative values to children. Therefore, the unpaid labor that women invest in the home regime to raise children must be treated much more seriously than the present literature provides.

The home regime is the epicenter of values. The values that we come to cherish as if they are our very own creations are in fact developed in the home sphere first. There, it is mothers who teach us what is deemed best, in their considered judgment. Mothers try to teach the important and fundamental value of discipline that is the art of controlling our unruly emotions. Once we master that difficult virtue, then they move on to introduce us to more complex values as we grow older. Thus we are subtly introduced to the respect of our elders, obeying their orders, caring for and being responsible for whatever is entrusted to us. When this model works well, the corresponding result is the disciplined self.

When we begin to mature, we are introduced even more to the intricate virtues of sharing, loving, trusting and saving. Note that these latter virtues are essentially economic. They deal with the practicalities of food, shelter, clothing and health. It is through the introduction of these material values that the home regime becomes a center of economic life. Preparing for major calamities such as famine and poverty are the activities of the economic virtues. That is precisely why great attention must be given to the strictly economic virtues, since it is those virtues, and the ethics that we develop by internalizing them, that either empower us to develop counterhegemonic virtues, or be so disempowered that we become victims of false ideologies that present us to the world as born to be poor.

The home regime is the sculptor of the self, and mothers are its educational forces. It is they who can make or break us, with the help of the transcendent. It is inside the home regime that the most crucial virtue of saving and planning for the future is learned; it is there also that the demanding virtue of saving through self-discipline is digested. The first few years of free schooling in the home regime translate into the birth of the economic self of the future.

All major civilizations of the past and present rightly spent billions of dollars to develop the economic self. So aware are child educators of the present that billions of dollars are invested on early childhood. That is why African educators also must pay maximum attention to early childhood, so that the economically disciplined adult can originate economic principles of social justice as they face the challenges of famine and hunger that are haunting the human condition in Africa. African educators of the home regime must know how to inculcate the virtues of planning and saving for the future with the intent of solving the poverty problem in contemporary Africa.

The centerpiece of The Famine and Hunger Project, which I have recently founded, is the systematic cultivation of an African economic and moral self, to spearhead the long-overdue fight against poverty and the inevitable consequences of famine and hunger.

FROM

Dekialula.com, June 7, 2006.

5 1

CUSTOMS AND CULTURES OF THE HOME REGIME

Households across the world have universal and particular features. All home regimes are the same in that they share essentially similar conceptions of the human self. That universal proposition about the two features of family regimes can be summarized syllogistically:

All human beings must be fed, sheltered, clothed and kept healthy. Africans are human beings. Therefore, Africans should be fed, sheltered, clothed and kept healthy. We can call that proposition A. Proposition A is a universal feature of home regimes. All home regimes develop ways of feeding, sheltering, clothing and maintaining the health of the individuals who inhabit the space of the household, or the home regime. There are varied practices and customs inside households that pertain to how family members procure food, shelter, clothing and health, the fundaments of the good life.

Ancient societies had no trouble securing the fundaments for their family members. The fundaments were abundant and individual members did not have to resort to reckless competition to have access to the basics. Individuals somehow managed to hunt, fish and gather fruit and feed themselves by taking exactly what they needed without depriving others of similar needs. Needs were controlled by other needs. There was a self-generated system of self-control. This is not to say that primitive societies were populated by angels or perfect moral beings. It is to simply say that these societies were populated by existentially serious family members. (Please see essay no. 55 on existential seriousness)

African home regimes, as part of ancient societies, practiced proposition A in the above sense. Family members were self-guided moral beings. When famines struck, they would either suffer collectively or come to the aid of the famished and the hungry by sharing with them the surpluses that they had saved for rainy days. They were able savers and careful planners, who did not trust nature, but prepared against it, cognizant that droughts are natural phenomenon, which can be overcome by strategic/moral/rational planning.

Such planning required the use of moral intelligence conditioned by strategic planning. Moral intelligence and strategic planning were ancient practices of primitive societies of which African home regimes were a part. By using the resources of existential seriousness, they developed powerful ways of combating famines, when they occurred, and controlled against famine translating itself into permanent hunger in the form of poverty. A highly idealized reading of their practices reveals that every individual's life was precious, so valued was the individual member that very few went hungry.

The concept of Maat in ancient Egypt, for example, inculcated into every Egyptian's sense of self a profound definition of the person as primarily a moral being.

FROM

Dekialula.com, June 19, 2006.

52

VIVA LA DIFFERENCE

Differences are the spice of life. Functional democracies in particular strive on them. A long list of brilliant writers, including the late Poet Laureate Ato Tsegaye Gebre-Medihin, have idealized differences including ethnic and linguistic differences, as the hallmarks of authentic democracy. His powerful poems and plays articulate democracy as the fountain of the well-lived life, where individuals, parties and ethnicities do not have to apologize for their beliefs and convictions if they let others with whom they differ on profound religious, philosophical and moral matters do the same.

We need not be the same in order to be lovers, parents and friends. Although love, friendship and family are not the same, and their essential characteristics are different, what cuts through all three is the fact of difference—that there are differences among individuals within the bond of love, the tapestry of friendship and the fabric of the family.

What concerns me in these turbulent times, however, is the place of the dangerously important fact of difference among us Ethiopians as we seek to define the future of our historic Ethiopia, which is threatening itself with the inability to deal with the pangs of democracy.

The essence of democracy is political maturity, and political maturity is expressed by the way we deal with all those who inherently and profoundly differ from us. Those who profess the politcs of the EPRDF and those who are organizing Kinijit, which is a coalition of four existing political parties in Ethiopia also referred to as the CUD (Coalition for Unity and Democracy), inevitably differ on profound matters, and they have inalienable rights to express their convictions at the right time, in the right way, at the right place and to the right degree. When they so differ on matters of election, modalities of governance and moral convictions, their political maturity is not measured by how quickly they could kill their enemies by resorting to intimidation, the threat or actual use of violence, but how well they use dialogue, debates and amiable conversations either to sway their opponents or to outsmart them at the polling booth at the right time, in the right way and at the right political space.

Violence produces violent individuals, dialogue produces articulate democratic beings and debate nurtures tolerant citizens who live politics as a fair game. Notice for example how Al Gore accommodated George W. Bush when the latter won the 2000 U.S. election by a narrow margin. The love of country propelled Gore to reluctantly but responsibly congratulate Bush for winning the election.

If we Ethiopians are to nurture functional democracies, we have to learn how to accept defeat for now, refashion our tactics and better organize our like-minded followers to defeat our political opponents at the rendezvous with victory next time. There is always a next time and no condition is permanent, least of all political fortune.

I advise my beloved Ethiopians everywhere to master their passions and control the urge to use our contingent ethnicities as a battleground of hate, of violence and of the inability to accommodate differences through the art of dialogue, debate, conversation and exchange of ideas. During this trying time of famine, AIDS, bird flu and much else, we must exercise maximum discipline and not let our passions govern our reason. Instead we must cultivate democratic reasoning to govern our impulses, instincts and ethnic excesses.

We must cherish and actively promote the founding of new political parties, political parties that are open to all, based on the respect of differences of opinion, and plurality of reasonable and rational moralities, convictions, religions and philosophical doctrines. Surely the democratic tradition is new to Ethiopian culture, but its functional presence depends not on the suppression of differences but on their valued existence.

I say to my beloved sisters and brothers: Viva la Difference. Let us create positive differences and annihilate negative differences. Let us construct democratic citizens for the future.

From
Dekialula.com, October 2, 2006.

53

A Tribute to a National Poet

Death is cruel and time is impatient. Death spares no one. So it took away our poet, Ato Tsegaye Gerbre-Medhin, Africa's poetic father, the handsome man from Kush, the land of AtumRa, the Egyptian god of absolute beginnings. That is where the poet located his origin, the nerve of his being and that is where he rooted himself with pride and brilliance, and became the source of African pride. I remember the man from the green fields of the south and the tall mountains of the north; with those piercing large eyes, which look deeply at the world; I remember the big forehead born for thinking; I remember the shapely ears attuned to the quiet of the night, listening to the song of the trees, the loneliness of the mountains and the agony of the nocturnal beasts at night; I remember the busy pen chiseling words as if they were elegantly slicing Ethiopian raw meat; I remember the older poet leaning on his cane with grace and patience; I remember the courageous poet compelling Ethiopian regimes to speak truth to power, and challenging power to empower the powerless and the oppressed; I remember the poet telling the African world that it is the birthplace of humanity, the place where words first originated and then spread to the rest of the world.

I simply cannot forget this dreamer-thinker, this thinker-dreamer, born to listen to the music of trees, and to the sorrow of the silent majority, wherever he found them. This cosmopolitan mind traversed the literary sources of the South and North, with ease and felicity. At home with Shakespeare and intimate with Ethiopian classical literature, his pen coolly examined every poetic wisdom and historical document and presented it to the world with the curiosity of the scholar and poetic insight. Rare was this poet's discipline and curiosity of the mind.

The dreamer-thinker has parted from us, but not the echo of those words that described divinities; the ears that listened to the voices of our African ancestors; the heart that felt the pains of love; the eyes that surveyed the interiors of tyrannical regimes; the pen that pierced deeply the sorrows of the oppressed; and when moved by love, celebrated the Africanity of Ethiopia and the Ethiopianity of the world.

To the poet, words were pictures and the pen the documenter of the human experience. There are no places to which his bright eyes, his sharp ears and his steady pen did not take him, so the dreamer-thinker once wrote in "Collision of Altars":

> I am a Kush, and of this land of Ra
> On whose roots the first sun rose
> My body living
> As my head is true.
> Mine is unlike your hybrid
> Devious, little Sabean mind
> Where the quibbles of your Ge'ez tongue
> Outlive the living body by far.
> With us, the body has language
> The mind cannot speak
> Both live. Without the one
> The other is dead; and
> The one cannot live
> The other's complete life.

In his other work, "Oda Oak Oracle", the thinker-dreamer sang:

> We cry
> Only to join our hand
> Come
> Abortive cry against Darkness
> Come
> The truer the love
> The thornier the fate
> And the more reason to die Come darkness, come.

That is how the poet made words cry. He had seen it all. His restless pen penetrated the agony of love, the anguish of the human condition, the stubbornness of pride, the cruelty of truth and the forgetfulness of sleepy humanity. And yet the poet tried to save the world by showing it the ways of love, through the language of compassion and reciprocity. His large forehead accommodated pain and joy, hope and hopelessness, always regulated by the discipline of poetic thought.

Today the body of the poet is resting in Kush, embraced by the ancestors and drinking the infinite light of the African sun, where his body is living and where his head is true.

Africa's love of its thinker-dreamer and dreamer-thinker will never die. His body will continue to think in the darkness of the tomb, where true love resides, and where there is no pain or sorrow, but an eternal presence of AtumRa, the Egyptian transcendent, with whom Ato Tsegaye Gebre-Medhin has now joined hands.

> Life is short
> Art long.
> Pain, joy and sorrow
> You saw them all.
> Generations to come will sing your praises
> The young and old will drink from the wines of your
> living body.
> Your mind is true
> Your body is language
> Hail to the Poet, Hail to Truth...
> May God enshroud this extraordinary poet with love
> and peace.

FROM

Dekialula.com, March 9, 2006.

5 4

WHAT IS A FUTURE LIFE?

A future life is a chance to live the good life, or at least the acceptable life. This possibility of a good life can be secured only if the self is guaranteed a consistent access to the internal needs of the body. There is no self without these internal needs. Surely these are not the only needs of the self. But these needs are necessary conditions for the future of the self, including the future cultivation of other needs, other than the internal needs of the body.

Where these internal needs are absent, however, there is (a) no future, (b) no life chance and (c) no future with meaningful life chance. (a), (b) and (c) are anchored on the availabilities of fundamental goods.

Put syllogistically, the argument is this: The human self needs fundamental goods to maintain its selfhood. Famished bodies are deprived of these goods. African bodies are therefore denied of a future with life chances.

These fundamental needs are internally indispensable for the human body. Such needs are goods ABC, in which A is food, B is clothing and C is shelter. No human self can be said to live if it is deprived of these bodily needs. Indeed, it is when the self is denuded of these goods that it inevitably becomes susceptible first to preventable diseases precisely because the most basic nutrients are conspicuously absent from the body.

The amount of these goods need not be the same. Indeed, the amount can never be the same. What is the same is only the fact that the body needs an X amount of ABC. Whereas the quantity of these goods is relative to the situation of individual Y, the need to procure the necessary amount of these goods cannot be negotiated.

All Ys are therefore needy of ABC, relative to their varied individual constrictions and histories. African bodies cannot affirm their selfhood without these fundamental goods. Famine first, and hunger second, at least for those who survive famine, are precisely deprivations of these goods of selfhood.

Thus the quantity of goods ABC is relative to the nature of individual Y. The procuring of all the goods, however, cannot be negotiated, whereas the amount of these goods can be reasonably measured, during the time of distribution. A fair distribution of ABC is what we need to focus on, once the goods themselves are made available.

When famines devastate African bodies it is because these goods have been unavailable for years prior to the famine condition.

FROM

Dekialula.com

5 5

In a Mood for National Reconciliation

Nothing is forever. Neither love nor hate are permanent. Indeed, no condition is permanent; and we should always look forward and never backward. Our nation has withstood so much pain, so much poverty and so many wars, with dignity, the dignity bestowed on it by the mighty transcendent; and now once again its children are fighting. Our elders are rotting in prison; the regime in power is not so much gloating over the suffering of our leaders but is helplessly frozen in time, not knowing what to do, except emit flames of rhetoric that go nowhere. Ethiopia is enshrouded by the darkness of hopelessness, and our politics is swimming in dark murky waters. We need to brighten the lives of our people with the brilliant arrows of reconciliation. If the South Africans could bend the depth of hate by loving-kindness toward their enemies, we Ethiopians could do even better.

Now is the time for the leaders of this regime to think hard before they put our nation aflame. All the terms that the opposition sought to negotiate before it was rebuffed must be put back on the table again. Reconciliation, however, must take place in logical phases, if it is to have a real impact on the mood of the wounded nation. The regime in power must not only release all the jailed leaders, but also each and every sympathizer who has been unjustly imprisoned only because they exercised their constitutional right of agency, of principled political action, the right to protest and if need be the right to die for it, as a higher manifestation of existential seriousness must be unconditionally released. Justice demands this comportment from our leaders, and the transcendent commands this moral law sternly. I appeal to the leaders of the prevailing regime to heed the silent commands of the transcendent to put the nation in a mood for peace.

When the jailed leaders are chided for not retuning to the negotiating table, they have every right to chide back by arguing that they are not going to return to the depressed halls of the Parliament without first negotiating that all those who fought for them and who are wasting their youth in prison are unconditionally released. That demand is sacrosanct; it cannot be negotiated but ought to be fully satisfied. Once that condition is satisfied, then the opposition leaders and the regime will have to sit at the round table and redefine the rules of participation as members of the Parliament. The moral integrity will otherwise be on the line, if they leave their supporters behind to reenter the murky dark waters of legislative battles. The nation will be deeply grateful if the existing regime would regain the political sense it once had and release each and every person in jail and renegotiate everything that is at stake before the opposition would return to the Parliament and engage in decent democratic politics of give and take. I am for one in the mood for national reconciliation in real terms.

What are the real terms? The regime cannot play the fashion of prepolitical times of silencing and imprisoning dissent. When the opposition says the elections have been rigged, it must not simply dismiss the allegation and place it at the rim of death. That is treason. That expresses the lack of political confidence. Nor should the regime play the people of Tigray as a deck of cards to spearhead its racial politics. It must let Tigreans as Ethiopians choose any party they want. The EPRDF cannot be a national party and a provincial party at the same time. It must choose its colors, and let others choose theirs. It should not be a crime for Tigreans to join the forces of the opposition, if public reason propels them in that direction, for the right reason and in the right way. That parameter is the line that defines the freedom of the thinking citizen, the moral subject. Tigreans and other like-minded Ethiopians should not feel guilty for being members of the opposition, nor should the opposition feel unnecessarily suspicious when Tigreans and others join its forces. It must encourage their participation, and it must genuinely educate its members to embrace strange bedfellows, when public reason flashes the arrows of reconciliation and the fashioning of the people's party, a new Ethiopian party, a party of love, of welcome and of authentic embracing.

These and many others are the new terms that must be renegotiated in order for the mood of reconciliation to acquire a stable national characteristic. The question is this. I may be in the mood for reconciliation, but is the time right, or do we need to outline realistic phases that would bring the combatants to the negotiating table in realistic phases, if so what are the phases? The next essay will seek to articulate the needed phases that must precede the mood for reconciliation.

FROM

Dekialula.com, January 5, 2007.

56

HEALING THE WOUNDS OF THE NATION

There is nothing that cannot be healed by time. However even time itself does not forgive easily. The current crises in our nation have hurt many hearts, and deeply scarred mothers and fathers, lovers and relatives who lost their beloved ones for nothing; even time, the patient healer, will not dare to touch these wounds and these afflictions. They will never be bygones. Unfortunately, these untimely deaths will be inscribed in the rituals of Ethiopian memory. As a people, although we are forgiving, to the extent that we can, we do not forget easily, however hard we try. This comportment is unique to the Ethiopian psyche, and we must live with this fact, with this national habit.

The current leaders blundered profoundly when they unleashed their guns and bullets on the voices of dissent, on the irrational and illegal pretext that the dissenters shook the fortresses of their sham constitutional order. What they perhaps did not know before they opened the gates of democratic voting is that the population had been deeply disappointed with their fourteen- year-old policies that it was a matter of time for the voters to let them know that unless they exact profound changes, they wanted them out of the way and to give other parties a chance to come up with alternative visions of governing this huge nation of seventy million people.

The leaders were genuinely shocked when the residents of Addis expressed their wishes by voting against them. The peasants of Tigray and beyond would have probably done the same, were they not intimidated and misled with ethnic slogans, and the demonizing of the opposition as the harbingers of murky ethnic waters of hate and divisiveness. That is politics as usual for some of the power mongers who are oiling the ethnic machine.

All these miscalculated steps are not going to be forgiven easily. The possibility of national reconciliation would have to be preceded by the leaders who must step down from the ladder of self-righteousness with the admission that the violence that was unleashed against dissent and the massive imprisonment that followed were unnecessary tools of barbaric prepolitical society.

Apology is a sign of intelligence and not a signifier of weakness as a generation of Ethiopians have been incorrectly taught. It is only the prime minister who could set this desperately needed tone of apology to be followed by the unconditional release of all the Ethiopians, leaders and sympathizers, who are rotting in prison. If the nation is to be put in a mood of reconciliation, an open admission of mistakes and miscalculations must first be instilled in the nation's wounded rituals of memory, before it is too late.

The first phase of coming to the negotiating table would have to be a heartfelt apology to our depressed nation. Great leaders do not hide themselves in the fortresses of well-guarded palaces from which catastrophic orders are aimed at peaceful citizens, they courageously come out and intermingle with the voters who once put them in power, and when they make mistakes, they either resign or admit their mistakes and persist on asking for forgiveness and move on to set a new mood, and new policies that would encourage time to send its wings of love and compassion.

Time, the great healer, could come to the scene to heal the nation's wounds only when those in power say they were profoundly mistaken and that they would like to leave a legacy of greatness and accomplishment by asking those who differ from them to join them in the setting of a new agenda for the Ethiopian nation's future. The unnecessary blood that has been spilled on the Ethiopian people's faces cannot be erased from the fabrics of memory. However, a great leader who could set the tone of reconciliation must first apologize to the nation in words and action. This disposition and nothing else can precede the possibility of national reconciliation. I call this the first phase. A heartfelt dialogue on national reconciliation could then follow.

FROM

Dekialula.com, December 31, 2005.

57

THE SPEECH THAT THE PRIME MINISTER SHOULD GIVE TO THE ETHIOPIAN PEOPLE

Honorable Ethiopian Ladies and Gentlemen:

I am honored to be the prime minister of this historic nation of a great and historical people, the people who inhabit the birthplace of Dinkinesh, our oldest human ancestor, home to the Great Axum, the originator of the first gold coins and obelisks; the magnificent Lalibela, where the most gorgeous churches prevail; the Historic Adowa, home to some of the greatest fighters who contained Italian Fascism; the green fields of the enormous south, which gave the world the aromatic and pungent Ethiopian coffee, not to say the sapientality of their proverbs, and finally, the birth place of Zara Yacob, the modern philosopher, pride to so many African thinkers, not to mention the lush, green mountains and plateaus that distinguish the Ethiopian topography by way of tickling world imagination. Indeed, it is a privilege to lead this nation. It is the sovereignty of this great nation, the constellation of magnificence that I have been chosen to preserve. May God help me to carry the task.

What is even more is the fact that I have been elected to lead some of the most industrious, patient and resilient people in the world. It is an honor to lead this historic people, who withstood Italian aggression, humbly continue to sustain themselves amid the ravishes of famine and the barbarity of hunger, always leaving matters in the hands of God, without ever giving up, but living in the shadow of hope and the possibility of redemption.

I was once young, a dreamer, a college student who opposed the emperor's neglect of the poor, who along with millions of Ethiopians protested the emperor's policies, and after the end of that era and the coming of Megistu's reign, my disappointment and anger continued and I joined the TPLF to oust the regime. I spent years fighting and dreaming to change the lives of the millions of Ethiopians who knew only hunger and early death. I dreamt on along with my comrades to change things and when the armed struggle ended, the Ethiopian people, with their characteristic generosity, religiosity and dignity welcomed us to come to the great Addis to bring in a new era of peace, development and prosperity. They patiently waited but the results were disappointing. Instead of peace, we gave them war; instead of nurturing the young treasures of their lives, we killed some of them. Hope is replaced by hopelessness, peace by war and prosperity by more poverty.

Our first few years were bumpy and peaceful, and the people gave us ample time to initiate change. We tried to change what we could. The change was slow, and our policies on Eritrea and on development did not move fast enough for our hungry people. We promised much, as young idealists do, and we delivered very little.

The war against Eritrea was a costly detraction, and I must admit that we made serious mistakes that could have been avoided if we had listened carefully to the advice given to us by our brilliant lawyers, but we did not, and the result as everybody knows is dragging us to another war. While recovering from that blunder, the democratic elections, which we thought were moving smoothly, had a shocking effect on our calculations. Losing Addis, where the urban dwellers live, was a total shock. We clearly misread the heartbeat of our voters, for this we paid a price that brought the nation to the brink of a civil war. Our pride got in the way, our mistakes revenged on us mercilessly. But defeat is not easy to accept, and we converted defeat into anger and anger into unleashing violence on our people. We literally ate our children. I too forgot that I was once young and impulsive, and should have understood and empathized with the urgency of the demands of the young who protested on the streets, and we should have known better than shooting at them. The mistakes have been done and deposited in the memory of their beloved parents and their loved ones, to whom I apologize from the nerve centers of my being.

How impulsive and insensitive it was of me to call those burdened by poverty and who had to resort to illegalities to survive "hooligans," how shameful it was to hunt down the oppressed and confine them to prisons, along with their leaders. I apologize for all these mistakes and ask the Ethiopian people to forgive me and give my leadership a chance to leave a legacy of positive imagery for the generations to come. It is so human to err, and so difficult but positive to forgive, without ever forgetting. We reacted too impulsively. I must admit that we responded not in the right way, or to the right degree, when riots broke out in the city. Blood was spilled; some important leaders of those who differ from us were imprisoned. I especially apologize to the committed leaders who fought for change, who are now imprisoned for the love of the country. May God protect their health and elongate their golden years. To them I offer the olive branch of peace and the ripe grapes of love and compassion. Please come and work with us. I am now ready to release every prisoner and am ready to invite the opposition leaders to work with us within the framework of the existing constitution.

Honorable people, I ask for your forgiveness and your willingness to give peace and dialogue a chance. I am ready to negotiate everything for the sake of our beloved nation. Making this happen is your call. The right to say yes belongs to you, as well as the right to say no. I will accept both. If yes, I will stay on and clean up the mess; and if no, I will resign in dignity. I ask all those of you who lost your children, mothers, fathers and lovers to forgive us, without ever forgetting the tragedy that enshrouds your life. I cannot forget the miscalculations and the mistakes that we have made in becoming the cause of the blood that was spilled in our people's faces.

Thanks for your attention, and the willingness to consider the possibility of accepting my apology to each of you individually and to the nation as a whole. May God impart his advice and put us all on the right path, at the right place, for the right reason and in the right way, to reshape the destiny of our historical people.

From
Dekialula.com, February 9, 2006.

5 8

THE PUBLIC SPHERE

The private sphere and the public sphere are the penumbras of political action. The private sphere is the intimate dimension of political life and the public sphere is the open fora to which citizens go to make their demands heard, to exact response from government and, most importantly, to develop political virtues such as obligation, duty, responsibility and civic participation. In the public sphere, our mothers play the indispensable role of teaching us to speak, to dare and to withstand the pressures of life. The fear of death and the consequences of courage are taught there, in the hidden school of the virtues.

The public sphere shares a family resemblance with the private sphere. Indeed these two spheres are integral parts of political action. They work in tandem, very much like theoretical wisdom and practical wisdom, both of which are modalities of wisdom, related but distinct, complementary but independent. What is true of theoretical wisdom and practical wisdom is also true of the private sphere and public sphere. In fact, it is the private sphere that feeds the public sphere by raising citizens and then after they mature, they resurface as seasoned political citizens ready to provoke action, and sacrifice their lives, if they must, for a just cause and for the elimination of deep inequalities. Our mothers are the queens of the private sphere and hopefully they will soon join the public sphere, where their leadership and counseling abilities are so much needed, and so ostensibly absent.

The public sphere is that political space in which the political self works with inclination, action and character. The political self's inclination for courageous action, sculpted in the private sphere, stimulates action, propelled by an injustice, a suffering, a disappointment that a vigilant citizen feels deeply inside her heart, and the citizen acts, and the action is repeated and becomes habitual, so habitual that the action becomes a living characteristic, and the political self evolves into an informed, responsible, dutiful and courageous moral/political agent. The public sphere then is that highly dynamic site of civil and political society to which courageous agents of change gravitate to put in motion the intricate relationship between inclination, action and character.

The public sphere, which is highly evolved in modern Western democracies, is conspicuously dormant in contemporary Ethiopia. The unfolding events at the moment do not encourage citizens to put in concert the relationship between their inclinations, their capacity to act and their wish to construct political characteristics. When they dare to act, they are cavalierly and capriciously accused of violating the laws of the country, and when their organizers try to train them to act responsibly, they are committed to prisons. Under such conditions the public sphere cannot possibly emerge anywhere. The public sphere in Ethiopia must be created. Without it, Ethiopian political life is destined to devolve to prepolitical times, as I will argue in "Waiting for Change" (essay no. 86), where I will distinguish prepolitical society as barbaric and political society as morally intelligent. The public sphere is the modern engine of political society; the public sphere is the arm and leg of modern democracy. Without a dynamic public sphere, democracy cannot flourish anywhere and at any time.

The web of inclinations, action and character that form the public sphere is being increasingly colonized by a mendacious tyranny that is literally eating its citizens, when all that they want is to express their inclinations, act on their thought impulses and feelings and learn at the right time, to the right degree and for the right causes of justice, the intricacies of political life. It is precisely the public sphere that must be created in Ethiopia so that the democracy project that we all want could be finished by the dynamic presence of Ethiopians of all stripes.

I invite women in particular to be active participants in the creation of the public sphere.

FROM

Dekialula.com, December 18, 2005.

5 9

THE OPPOSITION AND THE PUBLIC SPHERE

Boston, early winter evening, December 17, 2005, a night to remember, a gesture of the transcendent, who brought Ethiopians together on this eventful evening at the people's public sphere. All the way from a three-year-old girl to teenagers came to celebrate their Ethiopianity, and orchestrate their Africanity. Snow on the ground, cool weather and Ethiopians of all kinds walking stylishly to the public sphere.

My lonely eyes were swollen with joy. My ears sharpened themselves to hear the sound of the winter night. Ethiopians filled the floor to the rim. These were Ethiopians at their best. Young girls proudly swinging their hips to their self delight. They were not performing for anybody but themselves. Proud, confident and unselfconscious they surveyed the night scene with their large round eyes. The beautiful Ethiopian smiles brightened the dark night and warmed the human heart. Complementing the young girls, young boys were projecting their masculinity with calculated moves to attract attention. The exuberance of youth, the innocence, the fearlessness and the friendliness melted my heart away. These were young men and women with a mission to accomplish, although they may not know how, not yet anyway. Their hearts, therefore, their thought impulses and the life force of compassion were there as the potential content of purposive political action. These are the moments of energy, passion and interests that must be given content by the elders of the emerging movement. These spontaneous forms of revolt must be given substantial and meaningful political form by those who know, or who should know better.

This delightful night was organized by Kinjit. Done well with the company of seasoned singers, subtle poets and accomplished dramatists, the city of Boston rose to the sky, to the sound of drums, to the presence of the African body, the words of struggle and the yearning for change. The public sphere was used for festivity, joy, Ethiopians in concert, struggling to fashion a new party of the people, the people acting in concert, and seeking to redefine Ethiopia, this mosaic of cultures. Peacefully they rejoiced, quietly they protested. There was no violence or name calling. All was done in good jest, with political irony scoring points against tyranny. This was the public sphere at its peaceful best, and now the people in struggle and the leaders of Kinjit must move to the next stage of political action at the public sphere.

The next stage ought to be programmatic, with a systematically developed organizing principle, which must be found soon, or else all will be in vain. The most difficult stage now must be propelled by vision, by patient struggle and strategy.

At stake now is the place of youth in the burgeoning and buoyant moment of revolt in Ethiopia to be spearheaded by the leaders in jail. Central to that task is the freeing of the leaders of the opposition, soon before they rot, age and die unnecessarily. They will be more useful to the country alive and active than they would be as martyrs. Modern Ethiopia requires upright leaders and not dead martyrs.

The opposition in the Diaspora must now begin to organize struggle by joining the regime in power, and conduct massive opposition through articulating alternative legislation in the corridors of the Parliament relentlessly and concertedly every day. This decision must now be preceded by struggling to free every jailed leader of the opposition by working with international organizations, so that the freed leaders will join the government and fight it from inside. This move can only please and galvanize all those Ethiopians in Addis and beyond who voted for change. Their voices must be represented and not silenced in prison cells. That is not why they voted, and the opposition has the moral obligation to represent their dreams inside the Parliament where the existing regime will be fought against root and branch; and in the meantime, the leaders should train and educate their young supporters to take over key positions of power at the next ballot box, which is not very far away.

The public sphere should now be used as an arena of legislative struggle for the hearts and minds of the Ethiopian people at the rendezvous with victory, five years from now. Meanwhile, the youth need to be massively educated both formally and politically with a focus on the conquest of formal and political illiteracy that is haunting contemporary Ethiopia.

FROM

Dekialula.com, January 26, 2006.

60

WAITING FOR CHANGE

Pain. Death. Tears. Cries. Rocks and stones.

Desperate mothers parting from their dead sons and daughters; priests chanting peace; the young impatiently throwing rocks and stones; the police responding with excessive force; leaders commanding away from the comfort of the palace; the rich and powerful dancing at the Sheraton; the desperate and alienated sharing a pot of tea and whisking away flies in tea shops; sexual diseases spreading in the shantytowns inside dark tin houses— these scenes are the features of contemporary Ethiopian lives.

These scenes were the marks of primitive regimes in preppolitical times. Contemporary Ethiopia is indeed moving backward towards a prepolitical era. Shame on our leaders for taking us backward toward primitivity, when the masses cannot wait until they live genuine democracy, taste real development, feel the breeze freedom and flourish like healthy trees.

In contemporary Ethiopia, democracy has become merely a word, an illusion for the poor; development a sham; promise a joke; plans are passed by the times; existential seriousness a slogan; life meaningless; death a happenstance; food a rare commodity; hunger a natural condition; freedom a privilege for the rich; violence an instrument of intimidation.

These conditions must change. Democracy and development in particular cannot be realized through violence. Violence is a feature of prepolitical regimes. Primitive regimes use violence very much like animals do when dealing with their affairs. There was a prepolitical time in which regimes dealt with one another only through violence, when irrationality characterized the prepolitical self. Rational regimes on the other hand humanized themselves and entered the political sphere by using dialogue and debates to realize their goals. They use violence, when they must, with strategy and precision, at the right time, for the right political reason, to the right degree and in the right way. Violence is used for a specific purpose; of course mistakes are made on the way, and the leaders are held accountable for their mistakes. Mistakes are interrogated by the constitution and its able interpreters, the courts of modern democracy.

In Ethiopia, our leaders do not admit their mistakes. Not admitting a mistake is a virtue for our leaders. This prepolitical behavior must change, and it is only vigilant citizens who must hold our leaders accountable for their mistakes, and who must force them to resign when the mistakes endanger the future of the regime. The people must use their public reason and recall the leaders from positions of power. Leaders, no matter how they came to power, are not beyond the people-power to recall them when they commit grave mistakes. Just because they used violence to overthrow the oppressive regime that preceded them, they are not expected to use that violence against the people's legislative power to recall them for incompetence. If the future of the nation demands that they abdicate power peacefully, then they must do so, by way of paying respect to the sovereignty of the Ethiopian state.

Leaders must be willing to rule, when they are able and can, and resign their positions when they cannot rule and are no longer able. In prepolitical times, leaders would use power against the people who elected them, in order to stay in power; in modern political society, they resign their positions and give others a chance to provide alternative visions and policies. Democratic regimes use dialogue and debates to advance programs and political solution to political problems, through the art of compromise. The essence of politics is compromise.

FROM

Dekialula.com, November 28, 2005.

61

POLITICS AND SPACE—DEDICATED TO ETHIOPIAN MOTHERS

In the long history of humankind, particularly since the rise of political society, conscious citizens have been heroically fighting for securing a place in two spheres of political life, the private sphere and the public sphere. At issue in both spheres is the place of the vigilant citizen, as I will argue in "Waiting for Change" (essay no. 86), that whereas prepolitical societies used violence to prevent the citizen from securing a space in the public sphere, the citizen in turn continues to heroically fight for space both in the private sphere and the public sphere of modern political life. At times through revolt and revolutions Ethiopians and many others are resorting to violence and nuanced resistances to counter the violence that is being unleashed against them. Women in particular are organizing themselves to have a presence in the private sphere, which is what I will analyze below.

The ongoing turmoil in contemporary Ethiopia is no exception. The modern Ethiopian citizens who are conscious of their rights, are heroically fighting through spontaneous revolts, to make themselves present on the canvasses of the private and public spheres.

The private sphere of the household, the prayer houses and much else is intimate, sacred and hidden. There Ethiopian men try to rule by using the authority of tradition, and keep women in their place. Women want to be present in the private sphere of the household, in the interiors of which they sculpt children to become citizens; and men seek to make them absent by refusing to recognize their unpaid labor of raising children. Women in turn are resisting the subordination, control and humiliation by fighting back, and they are slowly but surely gaining space and becoming partners in this most important sphere. Some men are cooperating and rapidly becoming morally civilized citizens of political society. Other men are refusing to give up, and are rightly getting divorced and kicked out, and women are raising their children alone. In spite of some men's resistance of women's politically conscious presence in the private sphere, it is in this sphere that the heroic street fighters in contemporary Ethiopia were once raised. It is our mothers who teach us to fight fear and introduce us to the ways of courage very early on. It is they who systematically form our characteristics, the very characteristics that the young agents of change are using to resist the barbaric violence that is being waged against them. Were it not for the unpaid labors of our mothers, we would not have dared to sacrifice our tender years for the sake of making ourselves present in the public sphere of political action propelled by the imagination.

Now is the time to celebrate our mothers and daughters, the ones who raise us, under the humiliating gaze of oppressive men, unrelenting men, who use religion and authority to silence our mothers, who deny them the right to speak, to think, to organize, to decide and to deliberate. Our bright mothers are now using new interpretations of revolutionary tradition and religion to create space for themselves in the private sphere. For this mission to be accomplished, women must strive to fight illiteracy, so as to make themselves more visible and more powerful. Women's advocacy more than ever before must be combined with war against illiteracy. The private sphere cannot flourish before war against perpetuating illiteracy is fought. Illiteracy is to freedom as food is to the body, and education is to the soul as health is to the body. Our mothers could do even more if they are educated as to the nature of the biological self, so that they could raise their children as the doctors of the household. They have been doing their unpaid jobs well; they could them considerably better if they drink from the waters of modern medical education.

Not all fathers are oppressive. There were and are model fathers who enjoy the private sphere as the intimate sphere of love, of respect, of peace and of genuine partnership. We must celebrate these fathers also, and pray for their proliferation. Their numbers are slowly increasing, and if true change, for which we are waiting, is to occur, we must encourage this intelligent and constructive partnership to be the new organizing principle of the potential fashioning of the new geography of space, the public sphere itself.

I thank Ethiopian mothers and daughters for raising courageous men and women who are struggling to finish the unfinished Democracy Project.

FROM

Dekialula.com, December 13, 2005.

62

YEARNING FOR
POLITICAL SPACE

A woman in her early thirties, whose emaciated body shows signs of early aging, is sitting on the side road selling wilted and spoiled vegetables. She has sat there all day long, whisking away flies, chasing thieves and day dreaming. The sale of a pack of onions was the achievement of the day. All of a sudden, a neighbor drops in to tell her that there is a shootout on the streets, and that many teenagers have been shot dead by government soldiers, and she instinctively knew that her only son, a freshman at the University of Addis Ababa, must have died. Her son has been supporting the opposition forces for a few months. He and many others have been fighting for political space, nothing more than that. For that yearning, early death was the reward.

She was right. Indeed her only son, the treasure of her life, has been shot dead at daybreak, close to the university compound. With that death, her hope was taken away. He was her future. It was he and only he, who could have changed her life. She raised him as a treasure, proud that he was one day going to graduate, win a scholarship, and make it to one of the best universities abroad, and make himself a surgeon. This was the silent covenant between her and her son, and that is why she has been glued to the roads, selling onions and tomatoes, so that she could feed him when he comes home for the weekends.

Her hope is gone now. Her eyes are swollen with tears. Her empty hands are raised to the sky and seeking help from the voice and eyes of God. Tears flood from her vanishing eyes, those eyes, which had narrowed themselves from tears of despair.

Screams.

Tears.

Wailings circling the ground with the dance of death.

With the Bible in her hands, she wails, to no avail. Other mothers join her in this concert of sorrow, of broken hearts. Together they saturate the ground with screams of hopelessness, and inexplicable sadness, that no tears could comfort. As if that is not enough, her cousin, one of the organizers for the opposition, was dragged away from his comfortable home, whipped and slapped in front of his wife, and was taken away to prison, where his body is ebbing away with hunger strike. The mother is now saddled with the death of a son and the possibility of the death of a beloved cousin in his golden years, whom many describe as Ethiopia's gadfly.

Now she herself is on the edge of death. Despair is converting into dread, and dread into the wish to die, to join her only son, at that space where there is only a painless presence, a nothingness that comforts, an existence without space. This woman's life is a metaphor of the human situation in Ethiopia at the present time. Modern Ethiopia is burning with poverty blended with despair, life being navigated by fear, political action silenced by the ever-ready guns waiting to finish young and old lives, millions of Ethiopians secretly praying for the arrival of the Messiah to save them from the hands of unrelenting tyrants, the constitution waiting for a just interpretation by the transcendent and political prisoners giving their lives away by letting their bodies starve to death. Note, however, all that the agents of genuine change want this time to be is nothing more than space. The victims are merely yearning for political space. Is that too much to ask for from a regime that calls itself a revolutionary democracy?

From
Dekialula.com, December 15, 2005.

63

POLITICS AS THE ART
OF COMPROMISE

Christopher Clapham and Paul Henze recently combated
against each other in two illuminating articles on contemporary Ethiopia. Their arguments could serve as examples of the
need for compromise when two thinkers fundamentally disagree
on what their prognoses are of the current impasse in the Ethiopian situation. I would like to begin with a summary of their arguments and then proceed to present a view on what I mean by
"politics as the art of compromise."

According to Clapham:
- The Meles regime has been in power for too long, and it is
  time to look for an alternative.
- The prevailing regime has failed because it did not succeed
  in changing the basic structure, beyond entrenching itself
  in Tigray.
- Ethnic federalism and controlling political space through
  centralization are contradictory gestures that complicated
  the process of democratization.
- The government's decision-making process has been too
  opaque.
- The regime played off urban dwellers and peasants, and
  ended up alienating the urban dwellers which recently
  revenged in Addis, by voting against the EPRDF.
- The governments view toward dissent has been brutal, as
  was witnessed recently.
- In contrast to the prevailing regime's base, the opposition's
  base is heavily intellectual.
- The opposition's views of nationalism are underarticulated.

- The regime's attempts at demonizing the opposition as covert Derg supporters, Amhara chauvinists and Moslem fundamentalists are unimpressive.
- The leaders of the opposition are too inexperienced to develop an effective political culture to date.
- On the whole the elections were fairly conducted, although the regime did not expect massive opposition; voters conducted themselves with determination and calm; the results were complex; there was fraud and intimidation, which became apparent after the party lost in Addis.
- The regime has shown no signs of compromise or power sharing solution.
- The minister of information is causing the party a lot of damage by his neurotic behavior.
- The opposition is in a bind because it does not want to escalate violence but must also resort to violence to make itself heard.
- The government has an interest in presenting the opposition as violent.
- These dangerous politics in the end would alienate international donors and hurt the country. Clapham recommends that the regime leave peacefully, although there are no indications that it will do so.

In direct contrast to Clapham, Henze argues that:
- The TPLF leadership is that of honest Marxist Leninists.
- They adhered to ethnic structuralism; relied on dogmatic landownership; opened institutions; encouraged exiles to return; permitted independent press; established rule of law; and restored international relations.
- They built roads, dams, electric lines and telecommunications.
- They organized a workable multiparty system.
- The opposition is largely composed of Amhara chauvinists without a practical view on the national question.
- From the beginning, the opposition did not want to work with the existing regime.

- Henze recommends that the best course for the country is for the regime, which has a fourteen-year-old record of responsible leadership, to stay in power, as the regime that is the most effective to fight against terrorism.

I would like to navigate against these diametrically opposed solutions, and offer my own vision. My vision is closer to Clapham's but theorized differently. The African continent deserves modern regimes with the understanding that "no condition is permanent," least of all political societies, which in principle must be regulated by periodic change of power. Regimes of more than the lone individual ought to have an understanding of politics as profoundly contingent. Not only do we Africans deserve multiparty systems, but we need constitutions that promote a limited time period of rule, perhaps a maximum of two six-year terms, with a periodic election cleansed of fraud, which Ethiopia does not have at the present time. The ousting of tyrannical regimes with the organizing principle of domination and violence must be replaced by the development of humane democracies organized by the principles of uprightness, existential seriousness, dialogue and debate.

Clapham is right when he argues that overthrowing the Derg, and using the Derg as the epitome of a failed economic program, is the poorest standard of measurement that the existing regime could have used to congratulate itself as the model of success. The standard itself is defective and tragic, to be employed as a measure of greatness. Success can be measured only against the very best and not the very worst. Ethiopians should not be told again and again that they have been saved from the likes of the Derg by the heroic struggles of the existing regime. That is a very poor argument, and the Ethiopian citizen is yearning for a better self-defense. The existing regime does not have a superior argument at the moment.

That is why Clapham is right when he recommends that the existing regime should resign peacefully, and work more to leave a legacy of democracy with prosperity. It should make it possible for the citizens to have a positive memory of, what Henze has correctly noted, the fact that this regime built roads, dams, electric lines, telecommunications, permitted free press and sought to organize effective multiparty systems. In order for these images to linger in the people's minds, for the duration of its stay, the existing regime should compromise and share power with the opposition, in terms acceptable to both, for the sake of the Ethiopian people. As an African saying goes, "when two elephants fight, it is the grass that suffers."

When the existing regime kills, imprisons and the opposition is provoked to do the same, it is always the people who suffer. Compromise is the essence of a civilized political life. Indeed, compromise is the principal virtue of genuine democracy.

FROM

Dekialula.com, November 2, 2005.

64

THE NEW POLITICAL CULTURE

In my essay, "Existential Seriousness and Political Culture" (essay no. 56), I ask "Should their leaders be imprisoned and their followers killed and provoked to kill others only because they are engaging in a new political culture of imagination, of courage and a desperate search for a new regime, and a new political party?" The answer is no. No one should be imprisoned for articulating their rights and liberties. Rights and liberties are not subjects of imprisonment. They are the voices of fighting for life, expressions of existence. They are the everyday dimensions of existential seriousness. In that sense, they are inviolate, more precious than diamonds.

Moreover, the rapidly maturing new political culture cannot grow until the new Ethiopians on the streets are given the minimal political opportunity to fight against the law and order of the country by using their rights and liberties enshrined in the existing constitution, and point out the extremely inadequate realization of the ideals of the constitution. The existing regime interprets the constitution in one way, and the heroic marchers on the streets and pavements of the nation understand the same constitution in another way. They are correctly using the constitution to fight against the same constitution. At issue is not who is right, but rather why this question is glaring at our faces at this time, to this degree and for the wrong reasons.

The emergence of these conflicting interpretations of rights and liberties, equality of opportunity, the national question, the fabric of ethnicity—to name a few of the perennial topics of our time—cannot be answered by merely killing, imprisoning and intimidating all those voices of freedom and moral intelligence, who are sacrificing their precious lives, for a better life, and for the sculpting of a new political party that will realize their shattered dreams and hopes for generations to come. Their voices must be heard.

Their demands must be answered. Their dreams must be acknowledged and realized. If the existing regime can respond to voices, demands, and dreams only through imprisonment and mass killings, then that party has lost its confidence, and abandoned its constitutional duty of engaging the intelligences and imaginations of the agents of the new political culture. Therefore, the new political culture requires another political party, a party that takes the citizen seriously, and listens to the new voices of hope, of change, of new thinking.

The new Ethiopian reality demands the construction of a new political party or parties, which will contest for the people's voices and considered judgments. It is those who till our lands, who run our bureaucracies, wash and clean our clothes that the new party should listen to. They should instruct the party leaders about what to do and what they want, and not the leaders of the party who should command the masses to either obey or die on the streets. Any party that arrests and imprisons dreamers and agents of change is bound to dig its own grave. Anybody can persecute a new idea but cannot kill it. The same idea is reborn in a new form, at a different time, by a different generation of dreamers and social actors, who reinvigorate the same vision that was once brutally silenced.

Nor should the very young voices on the streets, who express themselves through rocks and stones, be dismissed as hooligans and robbers. They are not merely that, and even if they were only of that form that some look at contemptuously, they too have a right to exist, and the political party has the duty to reeducate this lost population to join the new political culture, as its new agents of change and transformation. A confident political party does not kill and imprison. The political party itself matures by recruiting new members from a wide spectrum of ethnicities, of language groups, of genders and classes.

A genuine political party is a moral educator, a teacher and a transformer, which teaches itself by learning from others, which matures by learning from its past mistakes. The existing dominant party has recently miserably failed to be a party of the people. It has become the party above the people.

FROM
Dekialula.com, January 16, 2006.

6 5

No Condition Is Permanent: A Theory of Toleration of the New Political Culture

In "The New Political Culture" (essay no. 90), I argue that we Ethiopians need to learn how to live with another under the atmosphere of political freedom mediated by a theory of toleration. No condition is permanent said Professor Anani De of Brown University. He is right; no condition is permanent in the lives of regimes. Regimes must serve and then leave graciously, and when and if they can, they ought to leave behind them a culture of tolerating differences, withdrawing from the political arena with grace and graciousness for serving the nation. African regimes come through the gun and leave with the gun, with blood on their hands. Should this trend be inexorable, or could it be changed by a new political culture of toleration of dissent on the streets, and debates in the Parliament? It is the political duty of leaders to embody in the nation's rituals of memory positive images that energize the young to build on memories of glory, of tasks well done and a confident generation of builders and thinkers, of upright leaders, and functional institutions.

Toleration is to freedom as love is to a true relationship of two souls under the frame of love. Political life is inherently marked by diversity of opinions, customs, traditions, doctrines, religions among groups, nationalities, ethnicities, genders and sexes of the human condition. Guns have a place in political culture. Political liberation, independence, decolonization and nationhood do require guns to dismantle the violence inherent in colonization and slavery. After that dream is realized, however, a new and difficult phase of political reasoning must replace the apolitical phase of overthrowing oppression and exploitation through violence. Our African ancestors have sacrificed their lives by originating the heroic duty of the vigilant citizen, which is the task of giving herself the dignity of liberation and nationhood.

The new political culture does not require violence but political reasoning built on the bedrock of tolerating one another and learning the civilized art of dialogue on the streets, classrooms and other political spaces to which citizens go to learn to be political, and to participate in principled debates on the halls of the Parliament, where the legislator reasons for the best policy, the best legislation and the interests of the nation.

The regime in power must set an example for the regime of the future and similarly the party of the future must correct the excesses of the regime it wishes to replace. If the old regime resorted to ethnic divide and rule, the regime of the future must not reproduce new ethnic divides; if the old regime resorted to harassing, imprisoning and killing the founders of the regime to be, the regime of the future must not ostracize the card holders of the prevailing regime. Their rights must be respected, and their preferences should not be trampled on. Their choice of A as opposed to B is an expression of a way of life, an ethics of existence. Indeed, they are pillars of existential seriousness.

The mark of a political regime in the new culture is not the number of citizens it has killed and imprisoned, but rather the number of citizens that it has educated as a moral educator and a trend setter, the trend of moral education through the art of toleration. Toleration is not taught through persecuting and killing dissent, it is taught by political reasoning, the reasoning of the public, through compromise, working out differences, letting opinions flourish and transforming themselves from the chaos of uncertainty to the gradual stability of political knowledge, knowledge as difference, knowledge as debatable, contingent and self-healing.

Regimes, like their members, must learn how to swallow defeat, when the best argument of the dissenters carries the day. They must learn to call A as A and not A as B, when A is the opinion of the dissenter, and B is the opinion of the power holders.

Regimes must accept their contingency. They must learn that they are elected for a limited time period and occupy political space for a framed time. They should not come to power to serve for life. Citizens need change, and when they ask for change, they should not be killed for it. Indeed, no condition is permanent, and similarly, no regime is permanent.

The will to change is what makes us particularly human. We get bored. We are experimental. There is always a mood for novelty, for trying out something new. For that feature of a new political culture to emerge, a theory of toleration that encourages and teaches dissent of opinions, ways of life, ways of seeing and hearing must be found.

The new Ethiopia desperately needs a modality of political reasoning that makes citizens sufficiently confident to speak their minds and fight for their convictions and allow others to do the same.

FROM

Dekialula.com, November 18, 2005.

66

CONSTRUCTIONS OF CITIZENSHIP

Sculpting a citizen is no easy task. It is an exceedingly difficult art, which requires talent, patience, endurance and tolerance. There are various kinds of citizens as there are regime types, fittingly appropriate for the citizen types. At the minimum, there are three types of citizens and three types of regimes that sculpt citizens. There are docile citizens; there are obedient ones; and finally there are (few in number, and getting much fewer in contemporary Ethiopia) revolutionary citizens. Ancient and modern and contemporary Ethiopian states have come and gone. Each of these states has actually attempted and succeeded in constructing citizens that perfectly fit their agendas. Thus docility, obedience and a revolutionary temperament have been carefully chosen and systematically constructed to produce the desired citizen subject.

The ancient feudal Ethiopian stage produced simultaneously a docile and obedient citizen subject, who responded to every whim of his or her master inside the house and outside in the fields and the production centers of the Ethiopian feudal state. A long string of brilliant Ethiopian writers have described this docile and obedient subject. A most famous novel, *Fikir Eske Mekaber (Love To The Grave)*, is worth rereading as a novelistic documentation of the construction of the docile citizen. Numerous historical works have also documented the same phenomenon.

Characteristically the docile subject of the feudal state did not use her agency to demand change. Fear of death and the weight of responsibility did not permit the heroic step of dismantling the feudal apparatus; in this the docile Ethiopian citizen subject shared numerous similarities with her other African brethren who were victims of the colonial apparatus that governed by using force and ideology to perpetuate itself. The Ethiopian feudal state also used force and ideology to intimidate any docile subject who even dared to entertain using her agency in the interiority of her dream space. In this sense the feudal Ethiopian state was exact and merciless in the sculpting of the appropriate citizen type. Obey or die was the motto of the feudal state.

Capitalist democratic states, as we have in contemporary Ethiopia, also use the same tactics as the feudal state in perpetuating themselves. Docility and obedience are preferred to the autonomous revolutionary spirit, which is theoretically enshrined in the revolutionary constitution of the ruling regime. In the beginning, the ruling regime, which sprouted out of the student movement of the Ethiopian 1960s, did mean well, when it gave a pride of place to the Ethiopian citizen subject, who willingly said farewell to docility and obedience, and embraced autonomy, disciplined rebellion and heroic agency to demand change and create possibilities. The revolutionary subject took her constitutional rights seriously and lovingly.

The revolutionary subject is always a thinker-dreamer and dreamer-thinker. For this revolutionary subject, as we witnessed in 2001, demanding a change is a right and duty, which she is willing to embark on, however grave the consequences. Also, the fact that the leaders of the ruling party were themselves at one point thinker-dreamers and dreamer-thinkers, who went to the battlefield to simultaneously overthrow remnants of feudal state, masquerading as Derg, was itself a catalyst, which emboldened the recent taxi drivers, the politically conscious people who voted at the booth and the student dreamers who gave their lives to do the same. The rituals of memory should enable the ruling regime to encourage the construction of a revolutionary democratic citizen, who can sculpt citizenship, only if she is allowed to protest, march, call for meetings and disrupt business as usual.

A revolutionary constitution should marvel at the construction of a citizen subject who shuns obedience and docility, and in their stead enshrines the virtues of autonomy and rebellion discplined by a revolutionary spirit. I appeal once again to our revolutionary readers to encourage the revolutionary subject to make full use of her agency as orchestrated in the revolutionary constitution.

FROM

Ben's News Page, Julne 3, 2005.

67

In These Turbulent Times

The industrious laborers of the north and south, who work from dusk to dawn, the fierce taxi drivers of Addis, the courageous students who, in 2005, sacrificed their lives for the second time in four years, the old and young citizens of Addis and beyond, have spoken at the voting booth, with a clarion and singular voice of despair, of hope, of anguish and of broken dreams.

The people want change. Now is the time to change. Now is the time to end the intense alienation of the past few years, ever since hope gave way to hopelessness, democratic protest to death in the shantytowns of Addis and constructive criticism to intimidation and imprisonment.

This is not to say that the members of the current regime, which embodies a new beginning under the leadership of idealists, some of whom were revolutionary students, have not put the country on a democratic path. Denying that would be a lie. They have exacted significant changes, but they did not stay on that humane revolutionary course, which their fathers and mothers dreamed about. We all change. Time changes. Time also changes idealists. This is what has happened in contemporary Ethiopia. The regime's impressively peaceful beginnings began to degenerate into tyrannical measures ever since EPRDF split into two factions, further complicated by the war with Eritrea. That is when turbulence began, and the leaders increasingly turned to hostile measures, when the wise and the concerned attempted to give them counsel.

I for one, exercising my duty and right as an Ethiopian, advised the regime through a series of articles in the Ethiopian *Reporter*. One whole year was devoted to the democracy project, which began in Egypt, passed through Greece and landed in modern Europe. Hoping that our intelligent prime minister and his advisors would read these carefully written pieces, as their counterparts do in the West, I poured useless ink and passion for five years, laboring away for free.

It was the love of country that propelled me to share my views with my leaders. I was ignored, and I remain ignored, but I will continue exercising my duty to my beloved country. So I write. What should we do now, when the democracy project, on which I labored, is suddenly aborted, and our country is devolving from democracy to tyranny and negative ethnicity on all sides?

Peace, patience and strategy are the genuine marks of revolutionary democracy. Both the regime in power and the well-meaning and frustrated leaders of the opposition are sadly falling short of possessing the above virtues. Genuine democracy is not built on sand. Building it requires the participation of the people in their quest at constructing citizenship. Any person cannot construct citizenship if he or she is not encouraged to protest, to revolt and to demand change at any time. A confident regime does not have the right to ban demonstrations after the people have spoken at the voting booth. Let the people protest, supporting the opposition. The opposition, however, should also discipline its supporters. The content of the protest must free itself from contamination by the language of negative ethnicity, which I analyzed in my essay "Two Concepts of Ethnicity" (essay no.39). I advise my readers to consult that piece.

When the members of the opposition resort to negative ethnicity and single out Tigreans, all Tigreans, as the source of the contamination of contemporary Ethiopia, this gives the regime the opportunity to do the same, and to mobilize Tigreans to defend their turf by any means necessary. In my "When Two Elephants Fight, It Is the Grass That Suffers" (essay no. 35) I appeal to the intelligence and decency of the Ethiopian people, to see through the machinations of desperate politicians to defend the interests of all Ethiopians, ignore sham ethnic politics. I say to the people, be wise, tolerant, patient and strategic.

I write today to rejuvenate that advice and add more. What we need now is a ruling regime, should it legally win the election, to change its ways. Gone should be the days in which serving in the liberation front should be the criteria of assigning jobs. Talented Ethiopians within Ethiopia and its Diaspora should be invited to serve their country. They should be formally invited to offer their services. Ethnic criteria and loyalty should be replaced by talent and responsibility, to be drawn from the rich tapestry of Ethiopian nationalities and language groups.

The people's votes are saying that the old ways are wrecking the country. Similarly, should the opposition lose this time, they should immediately embark on developing a genuine democratic alternative for their supporters. Again, the opposition should also focus on the criteria of talent and responsibility as they prepare the alternative program for the Ethiopian people. Positive ethnicity that respects language and customs of the mosaic of cultures in Ethiopia should be the future garment of the emerging new party. The Ethiopian people deserve political parties that stand for them, represent them and guarantee their rights to protest, change and transform Ethiopia, in their untiring quest of constructing citizenship. This is the duty of the revolutionary citizen type.

Let us celebrate the fact that our people have voted, spoken clearly and loudly that they want change. They are tired of enviously looking at the lives of the rich and powerful, when they themselves have not seen milk and meat for years. They rightly want to support a party that will secure them peace and prosperity. If the ruling regime cannot secure that, then it should not resort to violence and silence those capable individuals with alternative ideas. Central to that task is not less democracy but more democracy, not less tolerance but more tolerance, not closing political space but expanding it, not starving the people but feeding them, not less development but more development.

FROM

Dekialula.com, June 16, 2005.

68

A DEMOCRATIC CITIZEN

Aspecter of revolutionary democracy is haunting modern Ethiopia. In my essays "These Turbulent Times" and "Constructions of Citizenship" (essay nos. 92 and 93), I show how this specter has insinuated itself in the lives of the Ethiopian people. Students, workers, taxi drivers, humble bureaucrats wore this multicolored garment of revolutionary democracy and marched on the streets demanding their rights to be heard in. Many returned home safely, a few died tragically. It is the heroic students who gave their lives for their belief, exactly like some of their parents who fought against the mighty fortresses of feudalism and state fascism. What we need to hail is the fact that the first eight years of the ruling regime did successfully introduce the notion of lived democracy, democracy as a revolutionary comportment to modern Ethiopia's new political lexicon. For the first time in recent Ethiopian history, any Ethiopian has come to believe that he or she has some contingent and inalienable rights, expressions of existential seriousness. Some of these rights are the right to speak, to march, to assemble, to protest, to speak one's own language and to practice one's own customs, costumes and dances. All these new expressions of lived democracy were anchored on contingent values and further adumbrated by the essence of political democracy.

Consider the moral meaning of the death of students from the above angle. The regime justified its action by alleging that the students were actually looters masquerading as students. Let us grant the regime the view that it was defending the state from looters. But the regime is acutely aware of the fact that when masses of people migrate to the crowded city of Addis, their choices of survival are either (1) looting, (2) begging, (3) idling, (4) prostitution or (5) contracting AIDS and dying. A democratic regime comes to power to address these perennial existential and material issues.

The killing of citizens because of (1), that the regime is eliminating looters, does not inspire one to support the regime as worthy of its citizens. Neither the constitution that the regime engineered nor rudimentary common sense would hide a moral blunder behind using looting, which itself needs to be addressed, as a cause that is eliminated by unnecessary death.

Ethiopian citizens did not install this regime to kill them when they are suffering as looters, idlers, prostitutes and victims of fatal diseases. If the regime had ready to hand, concrete and consistent development projects committed to the idea that the basic material needs of the citizens (and not only the ostentatious needs of the national bourgeoisie of Addis), the dignified students who gave their lives would not have been dismissed as looters who needed to be eliminated.

Why do we have looters? is precisely an existential and developmental question that the policy makers need to address, now that they have secured power and, similarly, the opposition leaders need to start immediately to develop a coherent program of addressing all those complicated causes of looting, idling, prostitution and fatal diseases. I challenge both the existing regime and the aspiring political parties of the future to develop genuine developmental programs guided by existential seriousness and moral intelligence.

From

Dekialula.com, July 23, 2005.

69

THE IRRELEVANCE OF THE MILLENNIUM

Now that the exuberance of the millennium is over Addis wakes up to the empty tall buildings that could never hide the reality from 99% of the Ethiopian population. Ethiopia remains to be one of the poorest nations in the world. No skyscrapers can fool the vigilant eye from seeing the reality behind the veil of the millennium.

What is it that Ethiopia just celebrated? Celebration must have a cause. What is our cause? Reasonable people celebrate because they have achieved a dream, realized a goal and exacted a plan. Ethiopia has not achieved any of these, since the days of Axum and Lalibela, pillars of classical Ethiopian history.

Moreover, individuals celebrate their birthdays, if they can invite more than one person. In contemporary Ethiopia, only 1% of the population can remember when they were born. A majority of Ethiopians are born without knowing when and they die without knowing why, how and when. They die like cattle without a name, and without a history, anonymous and nameless; they leave no traces of their existence.

Here we live in an Ethiopia that cannot feed its population and that lives on handouts from the West, and yet we dare to bombard the world with the empty millennium, when millions of Ethiopians were stretching their hands for our refuse as Diaspora Ethiopians and local thugs danced away at our ugly hotels. How dare we display our ostentatious commodities to the eyes of the hungry and the famished on our badly fixed streets in Addis, a city built to accommodate 300,000 Ethiopians and is now infested with millions of malnourished Ethiopians.

How dare we display our American dollars to the hungry who will never eat chicken until they die? I ask you Ethiopians, where is your conscience and where is your political intelligence? How dare you stay put when your nation is burning in the crucible of poverty? How dare you celebrate on the backs of your people's backs?

From

Dekialula.com, September 19, 2007.

70

War on Poverty and the Empowerment of Poor Women

In the "Unconditional War Against Poverty" (Dekialula.com, January, 2006) I advanced several hypotheses, which generated powerful but short-lived responses. I should now like to comment more extensively on the idea of poor women's empowerment. Almost everywhere in the world, it is the poor who are stereotyped for being the producers of their misery. We say they are lazy underachievers, morally loose, without a work ethic and much else. Poor women suffer even more. They are absent in development projects. States hide them in kitchens where their presence is erased through absence.

The Ethiopian poor are not treated differently. In fact, oftentimes they are treated worse than their counterparts in the Western world, where the poor are sometimes given the opportunity to prove themselves through legislation that empowers them by making loans, acquisition of skills and seminars that show them the way of changing their plights.

Such desperately required medications of poverty are simply unavailable to the Ethiopian poor. Those who need them the most, poor women, are not even considered present. Present only in the kitchens of the rich, and on dustheaps of shantytowns, burying their AIDS babies, they are systematically disempowered.

This policy is suicidal though, because it is women who bear children, who make their children moral personalities, who protect them from early death, who teach them to be men and women and yet, they are not taken seriously as the house teachers. That is what they are, our mothers are our teachers, who teach us everything they know, everything they could know. Yet the extension programmers and the meager state monies never reach these women. Can you imagine what our mothers could do for us, if we in the Diaspora systematically raised funds, identified specific households at particular kebeles (Ethiopian wards), and made funds available to these women, the household economists, to disperse with these funds in the most appropriate way? I call this an authentic empowerment of women.

FROM

Dekialula.com, March 31, 2004.

71

THE MARCH OF
GENUINE DEMOCRACY

Do we have an organizing principle? I now answer, categorically; no we do not have an organizing principle. But we must develop one or more potent organizing principles, immediately; otherwise, the Ethiopian state, and for that matter the African state, will never extricate itself from the drama of human-made tragedies. We must stop producing self-perpetuating rulers with morally disorganized selves. All our leaders now are morally dysfunctional and must be fully medicated by Maat. Where they pretend to be moral educators they merely throw at us meaningless slogans about democracy, the market, corruption and much else; and we the sleepy citizens let them insult our intelligence by fighting among ourselves as we do in Ethiopia, Somalia, Darfur and North Africa. Shame on us for our docility, for marring ourselves in murky waters of destructive ethnicity.

By an organizing principle I understand a set of principles that motivate moral action and produce corresponding state policies. Principles become effective tools of moral organization when their content is substantive as opposed to rhetorical. Principles become substantive when they contain realizable ideas as opposed rhetorical ideals, which go nowhere. Ideas are realized when they guide the choices that we make as parents, teachers and political leaders. A nation without an organizing principle is like a self without blood. Principles are to the self like blood is to the body. The struggle for democracy requires principles, which are the nerve centers of political life.

Neither the regime in power, nor the the Coalition for Unity and Democracy (CUD), not even the emerging new parties have linked the struggle for genuine democracy with the foundational cement of organizing principles. Hastily erected five-year plans, ten-year plans or badly written empty manifestos organized by the principles of ethnic dirt and hate are no substitutes for carefully thought-out, plainly written principles, which can be digested by a literate citizenry and serve as the public reason of the citizens. The latter require the use of moral intelligence, the language of the human heart, as the seat of thinking.

The African continent itself, via the stellar contributions of ancient Egyptian priests, some of whom were the teachers of Plato, one of the founders of systematic philosophy, have already endowed us with Maat, a feminine symbol of justice, righteousness, tolerance, patience and compassion. We must integrate these powerful attributes as organizers of the moral and economic self.

I now wish to argue for each of the attributes of Maat by way of linking them to the struggle for genuine democracy, or what I have called the struggle for moral economy as the anchor of genuine democracy. These attributes ought to infuse the characters of the citizens and eventually function as mediators of public reason, the reason of citizens, out of whom we can then choose morally medicated leaders to govern us.

Consider now the role justice, a pillar of moral economy as an organizing principle of the citizenry in the formation of moral economy and the march of genuine democracy. When democracies are being organized, the focus should be on the moral development of the citizens first, and leaders second. It is the collectivity that must be educated both at home and later at schools, under the tutelage of literate parents at home and literate educators at schools, churches, mosques and temples. The march of genuine justice, the commanding principle of MAAT must be taught by examples; democracy is long, arduous and serious; it cannot be attained by rhetorical speeches by illiterate policians, appropriate models and the formation of morally enabling habits.

From

Dekialula.com, July 31, 2007.

72

Kinijit in Cambridge: Rendezvous with Victory

On a beautiful Saturday night, September 22, 2007, Kinijit and its delegates arrived at an Armenian church in Cambridge, Massachusetts. At this defining moment, the delegates gave a landmark performance to a calm crowd of over 200 people. This was Kinijit's rendezvous with victory, fated to announce itself in the next election, if the party disciplines itself and is guided by intelligent visionaries with democratic sensibilities. The accomplished lawyer, Ms. Birtukan Mideska, a model of reason and style; the polished statesman Dr. Hailu Araya; the brainy economist Dr. Berhanu Nega; the consummate politician Engineer Gizachew Shiferaw; and the shrewd strategist Mr. Biruk Kebede were there as founders of a potentially major party, thinking, strategizing, and resolving their internal differences to a very civilized Ethiopian crowd. Mr. Samuel Belehu, the master of ceremonies, did succeed in organizing a major event elegantly and smartly, considering the tension in the room.

Consistent with her loving personality, Ms. Birtukan read a public letter to Engineer Hailu Shawel, the official chairman of the party, who was conspicuously absent from the Boston event as a function of a widely rumored split of Kinijit into the so-called Nega/Birtukan and Shawel faction. She graciously invited the chairman to lead the party and to return to the table of reconciliation and dialogue. She addressed him affectionately as Gashe, the highest honor given to an Ethiopian elder. She stressed again and again that she admires and respects him, and wants him to lead the emerging party, the party of tolerance, the party of dialogue without domination. Her public letter was a model of love with dignity, of admiration of a job well done, of a legacy of service and sacrifice for an ideal, attributes that she so ably recognized in Engineer Hailu Shawel works for Kinijit.

The crowd in return heralded her name, and sang her praises, and she gratefully responded with a generous heart and an inviting smile. She brought the crowd to its feet with her contagious affection and her human goodness. The letter visibly calmed the crowd diffused the tension and warmed the hearts and smiles of the would-be detractors in the crowd.

The major speech of the night was "Development and Freedom." Dr. Hailu Araya delivered that speech coolly and systematically to a very serious crowd. Following Amartya Sen, an internationally acclaimed Nobel Laureate, Dr. Araya convincingly argued that true development must be grounded on freedom and the human self cannot produce its material necessities (food, shelter and clothing) under the condition of nonfreedom. He noted that freedom is to development as love is to a functional relationship. Where there is coercion, there is no development. You cannot fool people by handing them condominiums and other commodities to exact their obligations to government. A lasting development must be founded on freedom—freedom of thought, of speech and assembly. Given these freedoms, he argued, the creativeness and energies of the people will flow and propel the engine of development. For him, Kinijit aspires to be the party of freedom, the party that will devote itself to the preservation of the dignity of the Ethiopian person. He credited the existing regime, but not adequately. His party will translate some of the ideals of the existing regimes into practicable ideas. Freedom, for the mighty doctor, is the pillar of the open society that his party seeks to give those Ethiopians who will choose Kinijit as their new party.

Engineer Shiferaw's carefully crafted speech thanked the crowd for their relentless support of the party. He wisely addressed the sensitive topic of the nonattendance of Engineer Shawel as an act of a misunderstanding and a matter of different manners of work. He also expressed his gratitude to the Ethiopians who voted for the party in the recent elections, a point that he underscored when he briefly joined the guests at a dinner table and he sat next to two highly respected Ethiopian personalities in Boston, Mr. Getachew Selassie and Lieutenant Colonel Shemeles Gelaye and his wife, Fesesework Cheirent, while effusively socializing with them. He said, "The kindness of our supporters far exceeded the sacrifices that we tried to make. Our supporters were too kind to us." His interactive abilities with the guests was a symbol of the type of collective leadership guided by respect for the masses that the party wishes to give the Ethiopian people when it comes to power. This particular leader was open, humble and unafraid to speak his mind.

The voices of Dr. Nega and Mr. Kebede emerged in response to important questions on tolerance and the prospects of a fair and free election in the next round of Ethiopian politics. While reflecting on the theme of tolerance, a major topic in Dr. Nega's recent book (*The Dawn of Freedom*) written from prison, he joined forces with Dr. Araya's project, and presented tolerance as the second foundation of an open society. He impressively argued that tolerance is the pivot to the preservation of an open society, and that the mental development of the human being cannot occur, if the individual's freedom to speak, to think and therefore to grow, is seriously curtailed. For Dr. Nega, the dignity of the human person requires the necessary and sufficient condition of the tolerance of opinions, views and needs of the individual person. A major feature of tolerance is practicing the resolution of internal differences through dialogue and debates and not through guns. A repeated practice of these virtues will eventually produce the corresponding moral/political democratic virtues. An open society must procure toleration with freedom as the foundation of an ideal democratic regime.

Ms. Birtukan's public letter was an example of an appeal to the chair to return to the table of tolerance where differences can be resolved through reasoned dialogue.

Mr. Kebede's strategic abilities were evident in his carefully thoughtout counsel to members of his party. He teaches that building a party is hard work and that the ultimate forces are the people and not the leaders, and that the mobilization of the people for the success of the party is the key. For Mr. Kebede, important political virtues such as the loyalty of the followers can be secured only if the people actively participate in shaping their destiny.

Before the night ended at 12:30 AM, all the delegates agreed that the next election can take place freely and fairly only if Kinijit, as the emerging party, organizes itself effectively as the party of the people, not a party above the people. Expanding its base, and hence a function of its fund-raising plans, must be given a top priority.

Ms. Birtukan summed up the event by synthesizing the themes of the delegates, and stressing that a peaceful strategy of winning the next election is the singular purpose of Kinijit, the major Ethiopian party of the future.

The festive night was graced when the gifted poet Ms. Deberitu Negash, who is affectionately called Debere, hailed the gorgeous Ms. Birtukan. Debere's finest words of adulation were when she acknowledged how Ms. Birtukan managed to sustain herself behind the bars of the prison with such poise and dignity. "We are committed to you, our heroine—and we shall never leave you." The poet heralded Ms. Birtukan's name and the crowd joined the poet and sang the queen's praises, and thus ended a night that will go in the annals of modern Ethiopian history as one great democratic party of hearts.

FROM

Ethiomedia.com, September 29, 2007.

SOURCE

Berhanu Nega, *The Dawn of Freedom*, (Kampala, Uganda: MM Publishers, May 2006).

7 3

ANDENET (UNITY)

I understand the contributions of a mosaic of world historical civilizations within Ethiopia, to the formation of the modern nation of Ethiopia. The civilizations are those of Axum, Lalibela, Great Oromo land and the Southern parts of Ethiopia. The contributions of the South have yet to be carefully documented, but there is no doubt that they are there ready and waiting to be brought to sunlight. I myself remain curiously engaged to witness the disclosure of these momentous civilizations, so that I can add them to the extant list of the more known Ethiopian civilizations: Axum and Lalibela. Furthermore, Ethiopiawinet, I argue, is a synthesis of varied civilizations within Ethiopia, which have yet to be synthesized compellingly. I have not done that job to my satisfaction, as it is a research in progress. That the civilizations are within Ethiopia is not enough, some of my intelligent readers have argued, to compellingly convince Ethiopians that these varied civilizations that have been contaminated by negative ethnicity (NE) to experience Ethiopiawinet as a living moment of a untied people. My readers are right, the lacunae has to be filled, and in due time, I will meet their objections.

The hurt and the divisions are so deep that only time can heal us all, so that we can all willingly live as a united people of a historic nation, drinking from the fountains of Ethiopiawinet mediated by Andenet (unity) . So understood, Andenet for now is only an ideal, but once the wounds of NE are healed, Andenet can be a realizable idea. Ethiopiawinet, as I understand it, would have to be grounded on Andenet, for the idea to function as a vital force that can unite the Ethiopian people, who remain profoundly divided by negative ethnicity.

I had argued in Dekialula [Website], November 14, 2006, that:

> The recent explosion of the politics of ethnicity in
> modern Ethiopia calls for a re-theorizing of the idea of

ethnicity itself. The situation is so grave that it compels a philosophical intervention. I would like to argue that ethnicity could be viewed as positive and negative, which I would call positive ethnicity (PE) and negative ethnicity (NE). We need to salvage the positive merits of ethnicity, and avoid the strong temptation of divesting individuals and groups of the psychological and historically necessary need of investing in ethnicity as a way of defending the differences that mean so much to those who believe in them. The unnecessary contamination of ethnicity neither need nor force us to throw out the baby with the bathwater. The essential core of PE is the idea of   diversity. The attributes of diversity are distinctness of experience expressed in language, customs, traditions and ways of seeing and doing things; individuality; dissimilarity of experience; constructive articulations of unique ways of experiencing the world; and openness.

Those words retain their relevance, as I seek to explore their relevance in the ongoing discussions of Ethiopiawinet, which I recently called Ethiopianity.

Thusly understood, Andenet can be mediated by PE. Indeed, PE is the appropriate mood that united Ethiopians can bring to the palaver of Ethiopiawinet as they seek to proudly and positively share their customs, habits, languages and ways of life, as Ethiopians lovingly do at parties, when they are dancing away, unhampered by NE. When Ethiopiawinet insinuates itself within our veins, it readily stimulates our peaceful comportment and puts us in the mood for Andenet, or so I hope, in my attempts at a philosophical intervention through the tools of journalism.

FROM

Ethiomedia.com, February 20, 2008.

74

ANDENET IS SPARKING INTEREST AMONG ETHIOPIAN READERS

An anonymous reader wrote recently, "I share my Brother Dr. Teodros' call for reconciliation and renewal in the politics of our country as urgent and vital. I think it is particularly significant and heartening to hear when Dr. Teodros and others like him courageously speak truth to the regime whose top members, by accident of birth, happen to be their ethnic affiliates."

I believe that we need to be open and embrace Andenet as our only way out of the current political impasse. However, given the complexities of the problem, that is, the intransigence of the government, the ossified experiences and centrifugal tendencies of some significant opposition groups, the not-so-conducive international (security more than democracy) and regional (surrounded by authoritarian regimes save Kenya) context, the politics of Andenet won't be an easy one. I, for one, don't know how we can go about redeeming our country's politics in more tangible and practical ways other than thinking that, perhaps, some crucial ideas to guide such practice can be garnered by organizing a group or groups of able minds (compatriots and expatriats, why not Kofi Annan, Desmond Tutu and others for us too?) or intellectuals who can enhance the cross-talk among the various groups in the country in a bid to ward off any impending disaster and bring about the much-desired Andenet of peaceful change.

In order to realize this, I am sure that you will concur with me when I say that one needs a lot of faith, hope and courage.

I am heart-warmed by this response; may God proliferate such well-thought-out responses among my readers, so that we

Ethiopians could move forward, and in concert refine the complex politics of Andenet.

Andenet is an ideal. To convert it into a pragmatic idea that could take us to refine the politics of impasse, we must flesh out the content of Andenet. That is my goal in this short piece, which I hope other able thinkers could polish, on behalf of the Ethiopian people. First and foremost, what we need to do is to found an organization under which we can subsume the nationwide interests of individuals, ethnics and religious groups, under a single common good. Prior to that goal, however, it is of importance for all Ethiopians to cleanse themselves of hate, of suspicion, of revenge and other prepolitical matters and come to the democratic arena guided by a single idea, the love of Ethiopia, and the commitment and passion that cement that love. This imperative can be done only by Ethiopian individuals. The common good must further be cemented by a "general will," the will of every Ehtiopian, sufficiently general to serve as the will of the entire nation, minus the disparate and antagonistic wills of atomized Ethiopians. Andenet must be guided by the political imperative of the general will. That is the foundational imperative, and there are more.

As the anonymous, perceptive reader put it, we must anchor our agenda on hope, faith and courage. The second political imperative then is a blend of hope, of faith and courage, and of this three, courage is a distinct political imperative, whereas hope and faith are moral imperatives. The general will requires a political imperative for it to serve as a strategic mediator between vision and action. Courage is precisely that political mediator that gives life and movement to the general will of the Ethiopian people.

The third political imperative is the decision that the cleansed Ethiopian individuals must make, when they decide to put away differences and bring similarities to the forefront as they launch a social movement propelled by peaceful struggle as the struggle proper of political and moral individuals, who say no to unjust laws, who refuse to be docile, who put their lives on line for the sake of sculpting a new Ethiopia, as the blend of classical and modern Ethiopian personality.

FROM

Ethiomedi.com, March 15, 2008.

75

ANDENET AND
THE POLITICAL
IMAGINARY OF ADWA

In a recent sparkling piece replete with the remembrance of Adwa (the 1896 battle site defending Ethiopian sovereignty), Dr. Maimire Mennasemay wrote, "In 1896, Ethiopians of all origins thwarted Italy's effort to advance its colonial interests by fomenting ethnic hatred and pitting Ethiopians against Ethiopians. From Wellega to Tigrai, from Harrar to Gojjam, and from every corner of the country, Ethiopians joined hands with each other and Emperor Menelik to fight the threat of colonial oppression. Many who had serious disagreements with the emperor put aside their misgivings and sided with him. Even those who suffered at his hands rose above their pains and stood with him to defend Ethiopia's independence. Menelik on his part welcomed with open arms those who for years were opposed to him" (Ethiomedia, February 29, 2008).

Dr. Mennasemay is indeed right. Adwa is impregnated with a political imaginary, which the opposition ought to use as the source of data for engaging Andenet to propel the hidden force of Ethiopiawinet and stimulate Ethiopians to come to the democratic palaver and force the prevailing either to save Ethiopia through a peaceful struggle or abdicate power by the people's social movement.

I would like to engage the meaning of Adwa on three levels. (1) Emperor Menelik (1889-1930) as a uniting sovereign, (2) overcoming internal oppression through Ethiopiwinet and (3) Andenet and reconciliation.

First, Menelik was a shrewd sovereign, who intuitively did what he had to in order to save Ethiopia from foreign aggression. In the language of Maat, the African female principle of governance through political goodness informed by compassion and uprightness, the emperor managed to control his ego and engage his former rivals and enemies and invited them to join him to overcome a deadly enemy. He appealed to the people for help, for understanding, and the people joined him to do the work. The emperor himself internalized reconciliatory comportment and put himself in the mood of work guided by Ethiopia's common good. It is precisely this kind of shrewdness that the prevailing sovereign in Ethiopia is desperately lacking. The prevailing leader is intent on rejecting reconciliation and intent on doing everything by Orwellian political cruelty and a short-lived arrogance that would once come to haunt it. We do not have a sovereign of Menelik's quality, but we must develop one. For example, the Kenyans are on the verge of using the idea of the imaginary at Adwa and share power for the sake of saving Kenya from the course of self-destruction. Their sovereign leaders are thinking for the future of the country, and not their own future. Such is the fabric out of which true sovereigns are made. We Ethiopians should do the same.

Second, as members of ethnic groups aiming at cutting each other's throats, we unconsciously put ourselves on a mood for war. This comportment is neither shrewd nor wise, as it is nothing more than the internalization of the tyrant inside us, the tyrant of irrationality. We Ethiopians must work hard to cleanse ourselves of this devilish attitude that will destroy the Ethiopia that we all love. We must learn to forgive by healing the wounds of hate. The self-imposed, "internal oppression" can be overcome only by the oppressed. This kind of oppression requires time and serious effort and concentration to be worked on. All of us Ethiopians must first make up our minds to start the work in our private time. That is only the beginning, but a very foundational beginning for the larger political project of Andenet to begin.

Third, once the cleansed Ethiopian individual is available, then the political work of Andenet will place itself as our new project, a project I propose that the newly formed Ethiopian Forum of Solidarity can accept as a working manifesto.

The battle at Adwa is sending its wings toward modern Ethiopia and signaling to us that we will either perish or flourish; if we choose the latter, then we must use the political imaginary of the sovereign at Adwa.

FROM

Ethiomedia.com, January 23, 2008.

76

RECONCILIATION AND CHANGE ARE THE LANGUAGES OF ANDENET

In "Andenet and The Political Imaginary at Adwa" (essay no. 101), I promise my readers that I will attend to the third level of the meaning of Adwa, as I attempt to do now.

A group of Ethiopian friends are sitting at a café, and conducting a passionate debate on the Ethiopian millennium. One of them says, "The millennium! When we have more pressing problems rocking our souls. The shantytown around the Sheraton, the deadly dust eating Addis, the resentful eyes looking at the rich and powerful dancing away with their bloated stomachs. We have all these to worry about man." He sighs and adds, "Give me a break! What a millennium? When the nation is soaking in poverty?"

The young woman says, "Come on, face it, you are really resentful that the leaders are purportedly Tigrean. You have never accepted the fact Tigreans are in power. You would never lament, if your *wogenochu* (your ethnic group) were running the show. All this bickering is racist." The guy bangs the table in anger, and storms out of the café.

At the far end of the café, two older gentlemen are discussing the case of Seeye Abraha, and the fact that some writers are presenting him as a reborn unifier. Both gentlemen conclude that this could not be, that Seeye was once a murderer and that he will always be a murderer.

Conversations and scenes like the above are signs of a nation with traumatized and angry Ethiopians, for whom any talk of Andenet is a pipe dream, and a political trick by a few Tigrean intellectuals, the double agents of the prevailing regime. Yet,

Andenet as a political program is meant to be an answer to what Mikael Deribe pointed out in an eye-catching article, when he pointed out that ethnicity is a tool that the regime is using to prevent the possibility of an open discussion of perennial issues, for which Ethiopians should not be ethnically labeled when they express outrage and disappointment with the handling of certain matters. In his own words,

> My dear Ethiopians: there is a misconception of power within our society. The current regime has successfully tied power or leadership of the country with a privilege that comes with one's ethnicity. For a long time, Amharic and Tigrigna speaking people of Ethiopia have been portrayed as elites who govern the country. In fact the current regime has successfully blamed the oppression and atrocities of the past regimes on Amharic speaking people in general. This illusion has brainwashed some Tigreans, who have been led to believe that Amharas are indeed the privileged enemies of all other Ethiopians.

Through their ethnic federalism, the few elites in EPRDF have convinced Ethiopians that the people of Tigray are now in power. Addressing a TPLF rally in Tigray, speaking in Tigrigna, Mr. Meles Zenawi told the gathering people: "I am glad I was born among you gold people, and I am glad I was not born among your cousins." Listening to Mr. Zenawi's speech, naïve people at the rally may not have understood Mr. Zenawi's witty way of psychologically shaping the mentally of the Tigrayan society, but it is a deliberate and successive attempt to systematically alienate the people of Tigray from the rest of Ethiopia. Once again Mr. Zenawi gave the Tigreans the illusion and preserved the reality of the misery of the majority of the Tigreans marred in squalor and poverty.

Mr. Deribe is right; we must learn the difficult task of separating myth from reality. Why should Ethiopians be shredded if they take a stance against hot-button issues such as the millennium, or the invocation of Seeye Abraha, to mention just these two topics, in which unity and ethnicity are being pitied against each other?

Genuine reconciliation is premised on the possibility of forgiving mistakes without ever forgetting the meaning of the event in one's life. Remembering is a responsibility and forgiving the hurt and trauma that remembrance triggers is a moral obligation of the thinking self. We must learn how to forgive without ever, ever forgetting.

We Ethiopians should embrace Andenet not because we must forget the ethnic-based politics of the past sixteen years; we should embrace Andenet in order to save the motherland from hate and ultimate destruction.

FROM

Ethiomedia.com, February 10, 2008.

SOURCE

Mikael Deribe, "Demystifying EPRDF's Source of Power", *Ethiomedia. com,* February 21, 2008.

77

UNVEILING THE ANATOMY OF DESPERATION

The current Ethiopian regime is increasingly becoming shrewd, manifest in its uneasiness with Seeye Abraha's transformative New Thinking, specifically Seeye's call for reconciliation and change. While the major Ethiopian Web sites have all taken the route of grace propelled by the moral engine of the idea of Ethiopianity, AIGA, who many readers of Ethiopian politics consider to be the mouthpiece of the tyrannical regime in power, is increasingly seeking to isolate Seeye and some of the dissenting intellectuals into pigeonholes meant to alienate the Ethiopian people from the voices of reason.

As everybody knows, Seeye's call for change is serious, generous and upright, and Ethiopians from all walks of life, tired of the venomous and divisive usage of ethnicity, are rising to the heights of social cooperation by using the idea of public reason, the reasoning power of citizens who are drinking from the fountains of hope and moral engagement.

By using reason in concert with will and conscience, Ethiopians recently filled the corridors of gatherings in Boston, Washington DC, Denver and Seattle, and they responded to Seeye's message with a resounding yes, and proceeded to begin organizing civic associations and salons of discussion wherever and whenever they can. These actions have frightened the regime, and it is sending its handlers to attack writers with the cheapest means at its fingertips. Needless to say, the abuses have not stopped the abused writers from the use of the of the silent power of the pen, thanks to the mighty Lord. AIGA responds to the actions of the Ethiopian people in concert by setting Seeye up as the voice of Kinijit, the archenemy of Tigray, and the puppet of the oppressive party, all at once. The strategy was to alienate Seeye from his Tigrean roots, and simultaneously frighten other Ethiopians from Seeye the hidden Tirgrean nationalist.

Note the strategy of isolation and fear. We Ethiopians however should know better. Seeye is a genuine Ethiopian known for his fierce defense of Ethiopian sovereignty, which he exemplified with a military lucidity, befitting the portrait of a disciplined general—reasonable, consiencsious and brave. We Ethiopians must unveil the strategies of the desperate regime resorting to desperate means.

FROM

Ethiomedi.com, January 27, 2008.

78

MULTICULTURALISM AT COLEMAN'S CAFÉ

It was an early evening summer night when I ventured out of Stoneham, Massachusetts, to the beautiful Somerville, where I lived for twenty years, until I moved further north and made Stoneham my new home for the last two years.

My years at Somerville refuse to vanish, as they are firmly implanted in the rituals of memory. The narrow streets around Davis Square, the bars and shops there; Broadway itself, with its streetlights, the public swimming pool, the newly built condominiums, the much improved East Somerville, all continue to fire my writerly imagination.

Coleman's Café is in East Somerville, owned by the graceful Mr. Fekade and his tireless companion, Mrs. Belainesh. They invited me to an opening of the freshly redone bar, a magnet of ethnics and nationalities. I found myself there during a lovely early summer evening. When I walked in with two American friends the café was in full swing. Customers of all stripes with melodic Irish accents, soft Ethiopian tones, modulated European and American English suffused the ambience of the place. Mr. Fekade was swinging from place to place, with drinks in one hand, napkins in the other and smiles in between; Mrs. Belainesh was turning out dish after dish, all by herself, and feeding thirty hungry customers at the same time, and neatly placing the aromatic African dishes on the elegant tables lit by soft tenor lamps, the finest names in lighting.

The new bar is a delight to see. Oak wood finish, finely chiseled shelves housing the drinks and a highly accomplished American bartender tending to the timely and subtly served. International drinks adorned this top-of-the-art café at the heart of East Somerville adjacent to the ever-self-modernizing Charlestown.

The moon was out, looking after the multicultural crowd. Customers gathered on the bar floor, blacks, whites, accented and melodied human voices congregating at the bar, and then descended to the dance floor, past the dining area and in and out of the delicately done bathrooms. They filled the place to the rim. There was no space that was not filled by happy souls. Many people were quietly admiring the classy interior; a few were chatting and evaluating the place; many were simply enchanted by the teeming crowd inside. Everyone was busily engaged. "I love that spicy beef dish" said a happy customer to Mr. Fekade, the owner, or Mr. D, as his American customers call him there. "Thank you for liking it," replied Mr. Fekade, in his characteristically mild way. An Ethiopian philosopher, Professor Dagnachew, was chatting away with Mr. Tadesse, the distinguished owner of Quality@Yourservice, at Union Square; the beautiful Mrs. Belainesh was complemented for her colorful evening dress, and she replied with a bow and flashes of smile.

The American customers made it known that this café is their home, that they feel at ease to eat, dance, chat and raise their voices, while heated philosophical discourses were raging at one table; ringing political reflections of Ethiopian elections were heard at far end corner; feminist analysis on the condition of African women took place at a strategic corner at a far end high table. The café was exploding with joy everywhere.

American customers were enthralled by it all. Mr. Fekade and Mrs. Belainesh kept on working away with touching passion, exuding hope and prosperity for Coleman's Café. I was delighted to be there as the wings of multiculturalism blew past my relaxed body and elated soul.

FROM

Dekialula.com, May 30, 2006.

TRUTH TO POWER: AN OUTLINE OF SEEYE ABRAHA'S NEW THINKING

A pensive mind seasoned by the gallantry of war and the maturity bestowed by time sits at a Starbucks cafe surrounded by a group of adoring friends giving him the company and comfort that he lacked while he was wallowing in an Ethiopian prison for six hard years. The thinker in despair, the fearless military hero who rocked the Ethio-Eritrean terrain, sat alone, weighing it all, and speaking to time, through the language of memory. That was Seeye Abraha, medium height, cool, with bright fierce eyes destined to see truth and compel the brave tongue to speak truth to power.

When I first met him in Cambridge, Massachusetts, I was star struck for a long while. Unable to speak, but willing to listen to this frail body, hardened by time, I sat speechless. Suddenly the mighty soldier thinker made it easy, as words began flowing out of him with a characteristic lucidity, befitting a statesman of good breeding. With a measured tone, given only to gifted orators, he said, "I have known you in spirit for a long time, and even read some of your articles in the Ethiopian *Reporter*…and I so much want to know the learned members of my country."

Thus begun my acquaintance with Seeye, and I had the honor of spending five days with him in Washington, DC and then attended a conference where he gave a tantalizing speech framed by thought and propelled by measured passion. He spoke at the Hilton Hotel in Crystal City, Virginia, to a civilized crowd of 2,000 people. "Ladies and gentlemen," he said, "I developed my country's leading party, the EPRDF; the very party that I founded has now criminalized me. I was imprisoned, but thanks to my loving people, who protested and wrote on my behalf, I am now free. I will not rest, however, until all those political prisoners who are languishing in prison are released, as there are hundreds of them. The regime falsely calls them hoodlums and criminals. I call them political prisoners, indeed, they are prisoners of conscience." He raised his passioned voice and added, "Please do not forget these prisoners."

Thus began the two-and-a-half-hour-long oration, stimulating from beginning to end. He recounted the brutal fact that although he is formally free, the regime is keeping him under a radar screen, his house is patrolled twenty-four hours a day, his moves are monitored with frightening precision, all those who meet him are afterward interrogated, his former friends, including those thousands of soldiers who secretly love the military genius, refuse to exchange a syllable with him. His former employees were fired when they refused to testify against him when he was falsely accused of corruption.

The details of his everyday life as he described them to various individuals reminded me of George Orwell's *1984*, particularly Winston, the main character. The regime criminalized and kept him in check through meticulous observation, and through minute observation, sought to inhibit his movements, his dreams and his ideals. Mr. Seeye is also subjected to the same harsh reality. Formally free, Mr. Seeye remains the object of the gaze of power. His freedom is incomplete, and he is now determined to convert that abstract freedom into real freedom in concert with the Ethiopian people. The speech provided Mr. Seeye's outline of New Thinking.

Before he turned the pages of the outline of New Thinking, he asked his brother, Mr. Daniel Yohannes, a famous ex-president of U.S. Bank—the sixth biggest bank in the United States—with a quiet and dignified demeanor to stand to an admiring crowd, and thanked him for supporting his family during and after the demeaning years of imprisonment. He made a point to let the audience know that he is now penniless but chose the routes of dignity and service to country, while working with Mr. Meles Zenawi, before Mr. Zenawi turned against him. Meles Zenawi and Seeye Abraha were two brilliant students at the university as well comrades in arms during the peaceful years of the tyrannical regime.

The New Thinking refuses to say no to power, no to docility, but says yes to political action disciplined by thought and fired by injustice. "We Ethiopians need New Thinking," he declared to an aroused audience. New Thinking seeks to draw from the values of classical Ethiopian personality: respect for tradition, tenacity, resistance and cultural pride. The new politics of cynicism, he argued, must be replaced by a new politics of engagement and hope. "I am very proud," he declared, "to seek to set new standards of political excellence with dignity and integrity, a politics that resists oppression by risking one's life."

Whereas the regime sought him as an example of what might happen to those who dare to speak truth to power, he takes great pride in resisting oppressive power through reasoned courage, and setting standards of political excellence.

Mr. Seeye says yes to life with dignity and no to prosperity with corruption. The new politics of cynicism, which is producing youth who do not dream, and dissenters who are imprisoned for their convictions, ought to give way to a new national party, which will sculpt citizens with dreams and the right to live them.

He declared that his freedom is not complete. He said, "I am formally free but concretely unfree. But I am committed to convert this freedom into a real one, with you Ethiopians. Together we can forge a new Ethiopia from the mosaic of its ethnicities and nationalities." "Furthermore," he said, "the new national party should use ethnicity positively." He advised that ethnicity should not divide the Ethiopian nation. When propelled by a clean heart, ethnicity can unite us. Central to that unity is the idea of a united Ethiopia composed of individuals with rights, the rights to dream, to dissent and to speak truth to power.

The regime preaches that it is democratic, republican and federalist. The regime is not any of these. The idea of federalism is used not to check power by dividing power into the legislative, executive and judicial branches, in the great spirit of the American founding fathers. Rather, the executive branch dominates the other two branches in order to centralize power into its bosom, and thus obliterates the inner core of democracy, and plants the seeds of tyranny.

Furthermore, the contemporary regime is increasingly becoming tyrannical and its citizens are gradually becoming docile. For Mr. Seeye, docility is contributing to contemporary Ethiopia's political malaise. He contended however that a new political land-scape could dawn if the following conditions are met.

Ethiopians must reject the politics of division and cleanse their hearts and begin afresh and learn new political virtues of listening to one another with respect and vigilance. Respect, vigilance and listening attentively must be practiced as new habits. A reasoned dialogue free of domination must address differences and visions. Ethiopians should busily participate in the civic spheres and develop organizing structures where abstract freedom could become real freedom that controls the excesses of the highly centralized state, which governs by intimidating and controlling political space through the instrument of a sham federalism.

Tolerance is the ultimate medium through which we learn how to live with our differences, and *mechachal* (tolerance) must be the goal of dialogue. We should learn the difficult art of learning from others by listening attentively and respectfully. Intolerance is precisely what is destructively contributing to our disunity and to the benefit of those who are governing us by dividing us.

The new national party is a party of unity through tolerance. He said, "A divided house is useless." The crowd broke into laughter, when he said, "I am sure you are in utter disbelief that these words of peace are coming from a military leader used to settling differences through the gun. But you must believe that I can also settle differences through reasoned dialogue," and that is how the military genius spoke as a potential statesman, and a seasoned politician.

The crowd loved the change. He told them further that he is a changed man, a man who will continue to learn from his mistakes. As he put it, "I will never say I will not make mistakes. I have participated in mistaken decisions that the party that I founded made. I will make mistakes again and continue to grow from them." This new tone appeared to be unusual to an Ethiopian audience, who has never heard a notable leader admitting mistake and willing to correct them every time mistakes are made. This too is a brilliant feature of the new party of the future. He assured the crowd that his stance on Eritrea separates the duty of respecting the Eritrean people from the oppressive regime that must be changed by force if necessary. He contended that the war against Eriritrea, which he commanded masterfully was aborted half way, but the regime in power stood in his way. Had he been permitted to finish the job,

Ethiopia and Eritrea could have been spared of reeling under two oppressors: poverty and war. He was prevented from finishing the job militarily by removing the oppressor, the job was half done and Ethiopians are now paying the price; similarly he firmly denounced the regime for its involvement in Somalia as a political suicide. He is committed to the combat of terrorism by other means, short of an entrenched stay, which is endangering Ethiopian lives. He cried in his heart when he saw dead Ethiopian bodies being dragged on the streets of Somalia. Mr. Seeye reiterated that the ultimate solution to the Eritrean question is a lasting blend of firmness and diplomacy, aiming at ending the poverty of the people of these two nations. He called this solution a win-win situation as opposed to a zero-sum game.

The speech turned toward an articulation of his goal, which he ably summarized into the following points.

1. He will continue struggling for the release of all political prisoners, including his brother, Assefa Abraha.
2. He will appeal to the regime to change its ways and revise its national agenda by opening the public sphere and encouraging dissent and allowing contestations and debates with a formidable national party.
3. His politics of forgiveness allows working with the prevailing regime, including its leader for the sake of national unity. He harbors no bitterness, and is willing to work with all those leaders who love the Ethiopian people.
4. The party of the future should use the idea of ethnicity positively as a source of national strength and not the death of the Ethiopian nation through the venom of using ethnicity destructively.

He ended the speech by stressing that engaging the regime on any level is like walking on a sharp blade, but that he is prepared to die for a noble cause and the new politics of excellence demands courage mixed with strategic thinking. He advised the Ethiopian Diaspora to use its freedom and use the media and pressure the regime to change its ways by developing a new strategy of putting up a united front organized under a national party. This vision cannot take place if Ethiopians are divided and boxed in ethnic group busily

one another. He further advised that Ethiopians must use
ssical virtue of tenacity to resist and fight oppression.

se dangerous times, which could lead to undesired results,
must give in to the politics of engagement and hope cemented on
principled resistance. He announced his plan to continue speaking truth to power by risking his life, if need be. He appealed to
learned Ethiopians and Eriritreans to forge a new unity and solve
their problems through reasoned dialogue, the centerpiece of his
New Thinking.

After the speech was over with a standing crowd, attention
was then turned to attend to sixteen questions by engaged citizens.
The questions demanded answers to concerns revolving around (1)
asking forgiveness, (2) the mistakes of TPLF, (3) peaceful struggle
,(4) the question of the rights of nationalities, (5) supporting
EPRDF, (6) federalism, (7) Algiers Agreement, (8) languages,
(9) the Tigreans, (10) the rule of law (11) Eritrea (12) nonviolent
struggle, (13) the Eritrean question and peaceful solutions, (14)
national party, (15) new democracy or a repeat of the same, (16)
individuals and nationalities. He addressed them fully.

Most of the questions were addressed by the speech but I
will highlight brief responses to answered questions and longer
answers to newer ones.

1. I have made mistakes, and I may make mistakes again. I
   made these mistakes as an Ethiopian, which is his own
   measured way of apologizing to the nation.

2. Tigray is part of Ethiopia and the pains of Tigreans ought
   to be looked at the pains of Ethiopians, and the new politics of engagement should expand our horizons and not
   limit them. We must begin to suffer with any nationality
   of the Ethiopian nation. Their pains and triumphs belong
   to us all. We must learn the arduous task of empathy and
   compassion.

3. The question of peaceful solution, foreign to most of us,
   has not been fully studied. We must study this method
   carefully and use it as a tactic of resisting oppression and
   minimizing human death through violent struggle.

4. The respect of ethnicities is not racist; it is a nuanced way
   of respecting Ethiopians as members of different language

groups and ways of living. Individiduls did not choose to be born to ethnicities, but once they are so born, then we must respect their ways. Tolerance of differences is the answer to the question of ethnic rights. Ultimately, there is no Ethiopian who is not blended with the Oromos who are spread across the spread of the nation, and this fact demands our respect. Thus the demand of the Oromos is not propelled by racism but grounded on the fact that we are blended with the Oromo people.

5. Supporting or not supporting EPRDF is an expression of a political right, and not a matter of victimization by the propaganda of the party.

6. Federalism as used by the current regime is a tool of controlling political space by dividing Ethiopia into ethnic spheres. Indeed, this particular use is manifestly a destructive use of ethnicity as an instrument of division that contributes to the centralization of power in the hands of the powers to be.

7. I have taken a firm stance against the Algiers agreement as a grave mistake.

8. Yes, EPRDF has divided the nation by using ethnicity destructively. Whether or not the Oromos should speak Latin will be discussed in the future by the Ethiopian people under the atmosphere of freedom and via reasoned dialogue, free of domination.

9. Tigreans are Ethiopians too. They should not be attacked for their ethnicity. Nor should Tigreans be denuded of their right to support other groups, other than TPLF. They are individuals first and members of ethnic groups second. Not all Tigreans are supporters of the existing regime by virtue of their being Tigrean. They have the right to choose Kinijit as the party of their hearts.

10. The rule of law is a sham at the moment. The very laws that the regime crafted are the same that the regime is violating. The idea of respect for the rule of law has to penetrate our national consciousness. We yet have to create a society governed by law.

11. I had no intention of taking over the Eritrean nation. The strategy on the behalf of both the Ethiopian and Eritrean

people was to topple an oppressive regime that is disturbing the peace, and negotiating a reasoned solution impossible.

12. The bombing of the town marktplace in Hawzen on June 22, 1998 was a tragedy for all Ethiopians.

13. Yes, the Eritrean question can be solved by a reasoned dialogue, which would benefit all parties. Both nations can gain from a peaceful solution that would allow Ethiopian to use the sea outlets and Eritrea to acquire a trading partner, a market for its goods. These arrangement and mutually beneficial.

14. There are Ethiopians willing and capable of building a new national party out of the mosaic of its rich ethnicities and nationalities.

15. The new democracy will have to blend the best features of what we have built and an insertion of the totally new that united Ethiopians can forge.

16. The rights of the individual and the rights of nationalities are part of a single democracy and we are lacking in both, and when we can, we must satisfy both conditions.

These are highly condensed versions of full answers to excellent questions asked by a critically engaged and peacefully inclined audience, which gave the brilliant thinker its undivided attention, and thus ended a remarkable conference on a beautiful night in Crystal City, Virginia, on January 5, 2008.

FROM

Ethiomedia.com, March 8, 2008.

80

MR. SEEYE ABRAHA DESERVES A BETTER TREATMENT OTHER THAN SURVEILLANCE

The Ethiopian regime in power continues to persuade the Western world that it is a democratic government, that is honoring human rights, thereby protesting against the passing of H.R. 2003 (Ethiopia Democracy and Accountability Act of 2007), the sharp-edged blade that is aiming at shaming the regime and exposing its undemocratic ways.

Reliable reports from Addis Ababa are bitterly sharing disturbing information about Mr. Seeye Abraha, the former defense minister, whom many consider is the living conscience of the Ethiopian community, whose recent public appearances have attracted a global attention as the new symbol of reasoned dialogue, and whose generosity stretched itself and invited the powers to be of the ruling Ethiopian regime to reform their ways and work with him on the idea of Ethiopianity with dignity.

Seeye Abraha recently returned to Ethiopia, after a highly successful visit with the Ethiopian Diaspora, who graced him with a hero's welcome. Upon his return to his beloved Ethiopia, Seeye's invitation for a reasoned dialogue has been returned with an Orwellian style of surveillance of his home, his whereabouts and his very walks on the streets of Addis Ababa. His presence in any part of Ethiopia is being microscopically observed.

I appeal to the regime in power to stop this harassment immediately, and also alert human rights watchers everywhere to closely monitor this particular case, and use it as a litmus test of how genuinely democratic the regime actually is, and carefully look at H.R. 2003 as the ultimate language of power with which to communicate with a regime that is refusing to engage in reasoned dialogue, the language of genuine democracy.

FROM

Ethiomedia.com, August 20, 2006.

81

WHY DO I WRITE?

I must begin by thanking all the engaged readers who have been studiously following my modest attempts at contributing to the debates on Seeye Abraha, whom I have called "the voice of reasoned dialogue." Some of my readers have called me names, ranging from "the poorest of the poor," "the super paid handler of Seeye's group," "the hidden agent of Woyane," and most recently "an Ethnic lord, who is promoting Seeye because he is a Tigre like him" and many, many, other names. I consider myself quite lucky to be attended to with such passion. I like the passion of my readers; passion is a revolutionary virtue, because it motivates thought. What I do not like is venom, because venom kills.

Be that as it may, I know I must answer my own question, "Why do I write?" I write because writing is my vocation. I enjoy it. But joy is not the only reason. I write because I consider myself a responsible citizen of the Ethiopia that I love from the depth of my veins. I do not write to please the public; if I did, my life would be so different. To the extent that I can, I try to write truthfully at all times, although that habit will not make me "the person of the year" or even lead me to the right job.

I enjoy writing from the margins, where there is so much pain, so much abuse, and yet, as long as my words flow from the depth of my heart, and are monitored by the transcendent, and the writing is right and beautiful, I will have obtained a sense of fulfillment that money cannot buy. My recent writings on Seeye are motivated by a single idea, and that is, at this particular moment in time, Seeye, the reconciler, the insider, who has decided to tell it all by risking his life, and correct the mistakes that the party that he and the other members of Woyane made, will save Ethiopia from the path of destruction. Seeye is a symbol of change, of a new beginning, of a new rendezvous with Ethiopian history.

I do not just support Seeye the man, I support the idea of hope, of peace, of democratic engagement that Seeye is calling for with a contagious charisma and depth of moral thought, and I do so as an Ethiopian, born to a Tigrean family.

My foremost commitment is to Ethiopiawinet with dignity, to Ethiopiawinet freed from the venom of destructive ethnicity and freshly framed by the idea of Andenet (Unity).

FROM

Ethiomedia.com, February 15, 2008.

INDEX